INTERACTIVE GRAMMAR NOTEBOOK

GRADES 4-8

© 2018 Erin Cobb
imlovinlit.com

Credits
Author: Erin Cobb
Proofreader: Josh Rosenberg

Carson-Dellosa Publishing LLC
PO Box 35665
Greensboro, NC 27425 USA
carsondellosa.com

Visit *carsondellosa.com* for correlations to Common Core, state, national, and Canadian provincial standards.

978-1-4838-4937-9
02-239181151

Table of Contents

FAQ/Getting Started Guide

Why should I use interactive notebooks when I'm already struggling to fit everything into my day?

Interactive notebooks should not be another thing added to your day on top of what you are already doing. Instead, change what you are already doing to accommodate interactive notebooks. As a middle school teacher, I was already having my students take notes in their notebooks anytime I taught new content (such as what is included in this book). Interactive notebooking took the place of students taking notes. I consider the time it takes my students to construct their interactive notes as part of my explicit instruction time. And, it is so much more meaningful than a lecture!

When students construct these 3-D graphic organizers and put the information they are learning into them, they are making connections and organizing these topics in their brains in a different and more meaningful way than they would be if I were lecturing or if they were simply taking notes. Furthermore, most of my interactive notes are organized in a way that students can study them like flash cards without having to go through the trouble of writing out flash cards.

Do I have to use composition notebooks?

Although teachers have successfully used spiral notebooks for interactive notebooking, I believe composition books are truly better. They are more durable, less likely to fall apart, and the pages are far less likely to get torn out.

Now, you can still implement interactive 3-D graphic organizers without ever putting them into a notebook if this works better for you. One teacher I met makes lapbooks for each of her social studies units. After she grades them and shows students their grades, she collects the unit lapbooks and files them. Then, she hands them all back before state testing so that students can study. If you're interested in compiling these into lapbooks, there are great tutorials on constructing lapbooks online.

FAQ/Getting Started Guide

Does the type of glue really matter?

Absolutely! I definitely prefer to use white school glue when gluing items into interactive notebooks. Many students may purchase and use glue sticks, but I do not recommend them for interactive notebooking. Yes, they're more convenient and less messy, but they will not bond the paper permanently. I always tell my students that we use liquid glue because it will stick "forever."

Not only does the type of glue matter, but the method of gluing also matters. Here's a tip I learned at a workshop: NO BREAKFAST PASTRY ICING. You know what I'm talking about, and your kids will LOVE this analogy. I even begin by projecting an image of a yummy toasted breakfast pastry and asking students if they've ever eaten one. Most of them have. Do you like putting on the icing? Most students will say it's their favorite part! Well, you will NOT be icing breakfast pastries in my classroom! This analogy really works to remind students of the correct method to glue items into interactive notebooks. Breakfast pastry icing will result in wavy pages and huge, sticky messes. So, what's the proper way to glue? Use small dots (I call them baby dots) spread about one inch apart. That's it! The phrases I use with my students are "just a dot, not a lot," and "baby dots," and of course, "NO breakfast pastry icing!"

How should I organize my interactive notebooks?

Before interactive notebooks, my students' literature notebooks were a nightmare! Now, instead of having a hodge-podge spiral notebook that contains many random things (and notes here and there), students have an organized reference book of everything I've taught them. It makes it easy to study now and easy to save for future reference. During finals last year, I asked one eighth-grade girl, "Where is your literature notebook? I told you to make sure it was in class today!" She responded, "I left it at home. My brother is in tenth grade and he was borrowing it to study for his English final." Needless to say, she did not receive the usual one point off for not having her materials. It is my hope that the interactive notebooks my students take away from my class can serve as valuable reference sources in the high school years ahead (and beyond!).

When you begin using your interactive notebooks, be sure to leave about 3 blank pages at the beginning for your table of contents. Every time you make another entry, log it in the table of contents. What a great real-world lesson on this text feature! See page 5 for an example of what one page of the table of contents looked like for my seventh-grade notebook.

FAQ/Getting Started Guide

In what order should I teach the concepts in this book?

I have included many lessons and skills that I teach to my sixth-, seventh-, and eighth-grade literature students. The order I presented them in this book is close to the order in which I teach these skills. Still, they can be taught in any order or sequence that fits your classroom and the skills that you teach! You can skip some skills, dig into others more deeply, and mix and match them as you see fit. Take what works for you and modify it to fit your own classroom needs.

Furthermore, not everything in my students' interactive notebooks is content. I also have students glue in their reading goals, records, and even instructions that I don't want them to lose, such as how to access certain websites.

Do I need separate composition notebooks for poetry, reading literature, reading informational text, grammar, and/or writing?

NO! My students keep all of their ELA interactive activities in ONE notebook. I can imagine that using multiple notebooks would create a nightmare of having the right notebook at the right time and gluing the wrong template into the wrong notebook. I have come a little close, but I have never filled an entire composition notebook. If we happened to fill one, I guess we'd just get new notebooks and start over, keeping the old ones around for reference! As long as we're logging what we're doing in the Table of Contents, it will be easy enough to find what we need, even if it IS all in one notebook.

What about bell ringers and/or daily writing entries? Do you put those into the interactive notebook?

NO WAY! I never have my students "stick" random things into their precious interactive notebooks. These notebooks are sacred and no kind of daily work or jargon goes in there. Everything we put into our notebooks is useful in some way. I put things into the notebook that we will need to refer back to at some point, to help recall information, and as a record of the concepts, skills, and strategies we've learned. Don't junk up that notebook! I have another place for daily activities and free-write stuff.

INTERACTIVE GRAMMAR NOTEBOOK
Lesson 0.5: Parts of Speech Overview

Purpose: Identify and define the seven main parts of speech and give examples of each.

Procedures

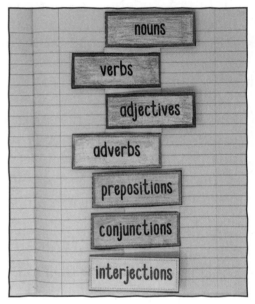

1. Start by coloring (I'm a color coder!) and cutting out the pieces as shown. It's important to cut out the little notches between each tab so that it functions right when it's put together.
2. Fold each tab over so that only the colored part shows. It should look like the photo.
3. Put glue dots on the back sections only (the gray *glue* sections).
4. Glue in both pieces, placing them close as if they were all one piece.
5. Notice that nouns and adjectives are on the right, and verbs and adverbs are on the left. This is to emphasize their connection, as one modifies the other.
6. Under each tab, write the definition for each part of speech. I use the most basic definitions—see the Notes for Template section. You may also choose to write examples on the back side of each tab.

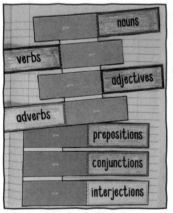  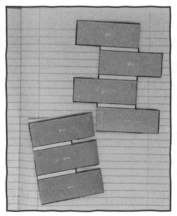 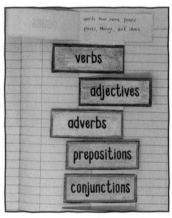

Notes for Template

nouns – words that name people, places, things, and ideas (ex. man, museum, leash, love)

verbs – words that express an action or state of being (ex. jump, hide, seem, is, are)

adjectives – describing words; words that modify nouns or pronouns (ex. pretty, brown, lazy, awesome)

adverbs – words that modify verbs, adjectives, or other adverbs (ex. softly, always, very, too)

prepositions – words that show a relationship between a noun or pronoun and another word in the sentence (ex. about, at, before, in, under)

conjunctions – words that join other words or groups of words (ex. and, but, or, so, yet)

interjections – words used to express emotion (ex. Wow! Ouch! Hooray!)

INTERACTIVE GRAMMAR NOTEBOOK
Lesson 0.5: Parts of Speech Overview

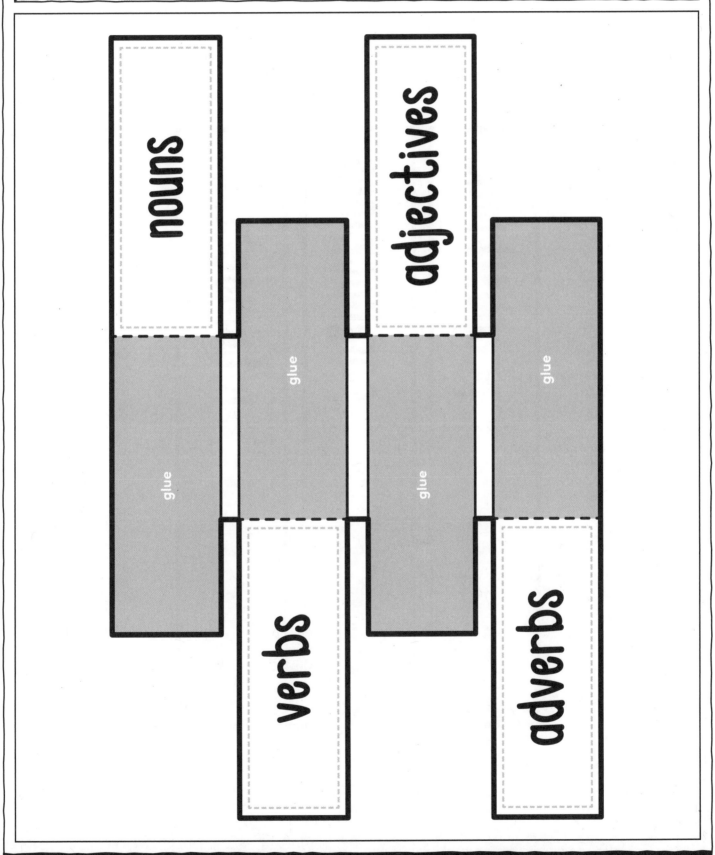

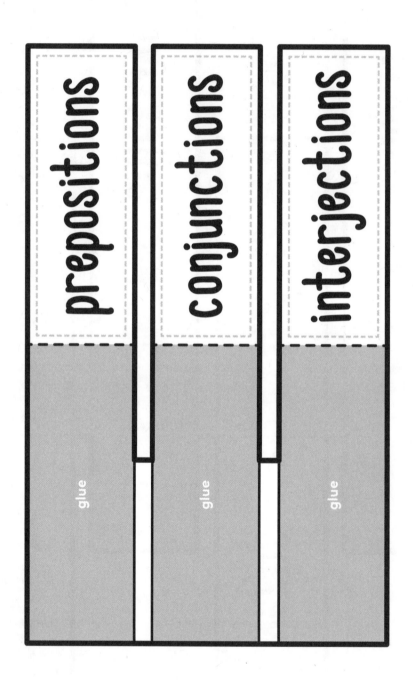

INTERACTIVE GRAMMAR NOTEBOOK
Hard & Fast Rules Teacher's Instructions

This unit includes rule sheets for the topics listed to the right. I spend the first week and a half on these lessons, gluing one into the notebook each day and completing the short practice activity. Students are not meant to master all concepts here, but should learn how to use the rule sheets through doing the practice activities that follow. We'll be touching on most of the rules, or topics, later in the year, and we'll come back here and list the page number where the lesson for that particular rule can be found.

The reason I start the year with these is so that my students can begin using their interactive notebooks for reference when completing activities like DOL (daily oral language) or other activities where they are correcting passages or sentences in their day-to-day writing assignments.

This book includes a partially filled out version of each rule sheet. It allows students to write examples in the space provided and record the page numbers as each related grammar template is completed. You may choose to fill in examples before making copies, to create a blank version so students can write in everything, or to change wording, definitions, order, etc. I've left a blank space at the bottom of each in case you want to add a rule.

I use the practice sheets to give students a quick exercise in applying the rules, but not so that students master all rules. That would be impossible in the first week of school. But, I want them to practice using the rule sheets as a reference. I like to glue the reference sheet on the right-hand side and the practice sheet on the left, but only after we have gone over all answers so that students are gluing accurate information into their notebooks. Use the Answer Key at the bottom of this page to check students' work.

Hard & Fast Rules for Using

Capitalization

Commas

Apostrophes

Quotation Marks

Numbers

Plural Nouns

Commonly Confused Words

Answer Key

Capitalization (page 11) 1. aunt, California, Golden Gate Bridge; rules 1, 4; 2. Dad, Wake; rules 3, 4; 3. Florence, senator, French; rules 4, 5, 6; 4. theme song, *San Francisco Spies;* rule 2; 5. *The*; rule 2; 6. My, What, Dad; rules 3, 4; **Commas** (page 13) 1. Germany, Italy, and Japan; rule 1; 2. Adolf Hitler,; Nazi Germany,; rule 3; 3. December 7, 1941,; Pearl Harbor, Hawaii; rules 6, 7, 8; 4. said,; rule 9; 5. treacherous,; rule 2; 6. However,; rule 4; **Apostrophes** (page 15) 1. Jeremy's; rule 4; 2. Don't; rule 3; 3. 1860s; rule 1; 4. It's, lions'; rules 5, 7; 5. James's; rule 6; 6. VCRs; rule 2; **Quotation Marks** (page 17) 1. My teacher said that it's important to follow grammar rules. rule 1; 2. Have you read the poem "Annabel Lee"? rule 6; 3. Mark shouted, "Call 911!" before running back outside. rule 2; 4. "Thursday is fine," Mom said, "for the birthday party." rule 3; 5. In class we are reading *The Crucible.* (accept underlining also) rule 5; 6. "Do we start school on Wednesday?" asked Cara. rule 4; **Numbers** (page 19) 1. twentieth century; rule 3; 2. eight percent, six feet tall; rules 1, 4; 3. The number of girls who signed up for cheer camp is 102. rule 2; 4. forty-one; rule 6; 5. thirty 20-inch; rules 4, 5; 6. 58th; rule 1; **Plural Nouns** (page 21) 1. kisses; rule 1; 2. toys; rule 3; 3. thesauri; rule 6; 4. libraries; rule 2; 5. hooves; rule 4; 6. embargoes; rule 5; 7. ashes; rule 1; 8. scarves; rule 4; 9. convoys; rule 3; 10. syllabi; rule 6; 11. vetoes; rule 5; 12. studies; rule 2; **Commonly Confused Words** (page 23) 1. affect, accept; 2. since, your; 3. principal, Who's; 4. beside, they're; 5. capitol; 6. It's, than

Hard & Fast Rules for
Capitalization

Rule	Examples	INB Page
1. Do capitalize the first letter of a proper noun—a name for a person, place, thing, or event.		
2. Do capitalize all significant words in titles of books, magazines, stories, movies, and other media. Always capitalize the first and last words. Do NOT capitalize articles (a, an, the), prepositions (as, at, of, on, for, in), or conjunctions (and, but, or) that contain fewer than four letters.		
3. Do capitalize the first letter of a sentence, even in a quotation.		
4. Do capitalize names of relatives that you use as the name you call that person by or that indicate family relationship when used with the person's name.		
5. Do capitalize a title that precedes a name, but do not capitalize a title that follows a name or is used as a general word. Do capitalize titles when addressing someone directly.		
6. Do capitalize countries, nationalities, and languages.		

Name _____   Date _____

Hard & Fast Rules: Capitalization

Each sentence contains mistakes. Use your "Hard & Fast Rules" sheet to identify the mistakes and correct them. Then, identify which rule(s) apply to the sentence.

1 On the way to visit my Aunt in california, we crossed the golden gate bridge.

2 From the backseat I heard dad shout, "wake up kids, and take in this view!"

3 Grandma Florence, whose other son is a Senator, started talking way too fast in french.

4 Then, I realized that this was the same bridge from the Theme Song to the television show San Francisco Spies.

5 My brother never looked up from the book he was reading, *the Triad Trials.*

6 my mother said, "what a beautiful sight!" and then she hugged dad.

Hard & Fast Rules for Using
Commas

Rule	Examples	INB Page
1. Do use commas to separate three or more items or elements in a series.		
2. Do use a comma between two adjectives only when the word *and* could be inserted in its place.		
3. Do use a comma before and after a word or phrase that renames a noun (appositives).		
4. Do use a comma when a sentence begins with an introductory word or phrase such as *well, yes, therefore, for example,* or *on the other hand.*		
5. Do use commas before and after a word used as an interrupter, such as *however.*		
6. Do use commas between a city and state (and after the state if the sentence continues).		
7. Do use commas to separate the day of the month from the year (and after the year if the sentence continues).		
8. Do use a comma when a sentence begins with a prepositional phrase, adverbial clause, or dependent clause.		
9. Do use a comma to introduce or interrupt direct quotations or after a direct question.		

Name _____   Date _____

Hard & Fast Rules: Using Commas

Each sentence contains mistakes. Use your "Hard & Fast Rules" sheet to identify the mistakes and correct them. Then, identify which rule(s) apply to the sentence.

1 During World War II the US and Allies fought against Germany Italy and Japan.

2 Adolf Hitler the leader of Nazi Germany was one of Europe's greatest enemies.

3 On the morning of December 7 1941 the Japanese attacked a naval base in Pearl Harbor Hawaii.

4 President Franklin D. Roosevelt said "The only thing we have to fear is fear itself."

5 World War II would become a treacherous bloody battle.

6 However peace was restored in Europe and in the Pacific.

INTERACTIVE GRAMMAR NOTEBOOK
Hard & Fast Rules: Using Apostrophes

Hard & Fast Rules for Using
Apostrophes

Rule	Examples	INB Page
1. Do NOT use for numbers that are plural nouns.		
2. Do NOT use for capital letters that are plural nouns or abbreviations.		
3. Do use for contractions in the place of missing letters.		
4. Do use 's to show possession when something belongs to one person or thing.		
5. Do use after the plural s to show possession when something belongs to more than one person or thing. Make the noun plural first, and then add the apostrophe.		
6. Do use 's to show possession of a name that ends in s.		
7. Its and it's are special cases. its = something belongs to it it's = contraction for it is or it has		

Name _____   Date _____

Hard & Fast Rules: Using Apostrophes

Each sentence contains mistakes. Use your "Hard & Fast Rules" sheet to identify the mistakes and correct them. Then, identify which rule(s) apply to the sentence.

1 Jeremys brand new fishing pole is already broken.

2 Dont overuse the apostrophe!

3 The American Civil War was fought between the North and the South in the 1860's.

4 Its a good idea to avoid the lions habitat.

5 My cousins and I went to see James' new lab puppies.

6 There are several old VCR's just sitting in the attic.

Hard & Fast Rules for Using
Quotation Marks

Rule	Examples	INB Page
1. Quotation marks should only be used for direct quotes, not for indirect quotes.		
2. Use a comma after a direct quotation in a sentence. Commas always go inside quotation marks.		
3. Use a comma to introduce or interrupt direct quotations or after a direct quotation.		
4. When a question is asked inside quotation marks, use a question mark instead of a comma. In a statement, always use a comma in place of the period.		
5. Use quotation marks for the titles of publications that are parts of bigger publications. The bigger publication is underlined or written in italics.		
6. When a question ends with a title in quotations, place the question mark outside of the quotation marks. Question marks and exclamation points only go inside of quotation marks if they are part of the quoted matter.		

Name _____   Date _____

Hard & Fast Rules: Using Quotation Marks

Each sentence contains mistakes. Use your "Hard & Fast Rules" sheet to identify the mistakes and correct them. Then, identify which rule(s) apply to the sentence.

1 My teacher said that "it's important to follow grammar rules."

2 Have you read the poem, Annabel Lee?

3 Mark shouted, Call 911, before running back outside!

4 Thursday is fine, Mom said, for the birthday party.

5 In class we are reading "The Crucible."

6 Do we start school on Wednesday, asked Cara?

Hard & Fast Rules for Using
Numbers

Rule	Examples	INB Page
1. Spell out numbers less than 10. Use numerals for numbers 10 and above. The same rule also applies to ordinal numbers.		
2. Do not begin a sentence with a numeral. To avoid writing out long numbers, reword the sentence.		
3. Spell out centuries and decades. Use numerals for years.		
4. Do not abbreviate units of measurement. Write out the word *percent*.		
5. When two numbers are next to each other, write out one of them.		
6. Be consistent within the same sentence with the same types of numbers, even if you must break the first rule.		

Hard & Fast Rules: Using Numbers

Each sentence contains mistakes. Use your "Hard & Fast Rules" sheet to identify the mistakes and correct them. Then, identify which rule(s) apply to the sentence.

1 Many wars took place during the 20th century.

2 Last year, 8% of students were more than 6 ft. tall.

3 102 girls signed up for cheer camp.

4 Only ten students passed the test, while 41 students failed it.

5 There are 30 20-in. monitors in the computer lab.

6 I counted to see that I was the fifty-eighth person on the list.

Hard & Fast Rules for Making
Plural Nouns

If a noun ends with...	Then...	Examples
1. s ch sh x z ss	add -*es*.	
2. consonant + **y**	change *y* to *i* and add -*es*.	
3. vowel + **y**	add -*s*.	
4. **f** or **fe**	add -*s*, or change *f* to *v* and add -*es*.	
5. consonant + **o**	add -*es*.	
6. **us** (for words of Latin origin)	change *us* to *i*.	

Some Common Irregular Plurals	Some Nouns Do Not Change

Hard & Fast Rules: Using Plurals

For each noun on the left, write its plural form. Then, use your "Hard & Fast Rules" sheet to identify which rule you used.

	Plural Form	Rule
1. kiss		
2. toy		
3. thesaurus		
4. library		
5. hoof		
6. embargo		
7. ash		
8. scarf		
9. convoy		
10. syllabus		
11. veto		
12. study		

Hard & Fast Rules for Using
Commonly Confused Words

Words & Meanings	Examples
accept – to receive **except** – with the exclusion of	
affect – to influence or change (verb) **effect** – result (noun)	
beside – close to or next to **besides** – except for; in addition	
capital – major city; synonym for *primary* **capitol** – a government building	
its – the possessive form of *it* **it's** – contraction for *it is* or *it has*	
principal – administrator of a school **principle** – moral conviction or basic truth	
sense – perception or understanding **since** – indication of past time; because	
than – compared to **then** – at that time; next	
their – possessive form of *they* **there** – in that place **they're** – contraction for *they are*	
whose – possessive form of *whom* **who's** – contraction for *who is*	
your – possessive form of *you* **you're** – contraction for *you are*	

Name _____ Date _____

Hard & Fast Rules: Using Commonly Confused Words

Read each sentence. Decide which of the commonly confused words following the sentence belong in each space. Rewrite the sentences with the correct words.

1 The accident did not _____ Sarah's decision to _____ the scholarship. (affect/effect, accept/except)

2 Ever _____ gym class, _____ shoes have been giving off an awful odor! (sense/since, your/you're)

3 The _____ asked, "_____ skipping class?" (principal/principle, Who's/Whose)

4 I put my glasses down _____ the book and now _____ gone! (beside/besides, their/there/they're)

5 We toured the legislative offices at the state _____ building. (capital/capitol)

6 _____ more important to study _____ it is to party. (It's/Its, than/then)

INTERACTIVE GRAMMAR NOTEBOOK
Lesson 2-1: Four Types of Sentences

Purpose: Identify the four types of sentences (declarative, imperative, interrogative, exclamatory) and the type of punctuation to use with each.

Procedures (Activity 1)

1. Label and outline the keys on the template. Write each type of sentence on the proper key. I like to use both forms of the types, so for imperative sentences, I also add *(command)* in parentheses. If you want to assign each type of sentence a color, do that now.
2. Cut out the template and glue the title on the top of the page.
3. Turn each of the punctuation mark keys into a tab by folding down about a 1/2-inch tab from the top.
4. Add glue dots to the backs of the tabs and glue them to the page.
5. Write information about each sentence type under the tabs. See the Notes for Template section.

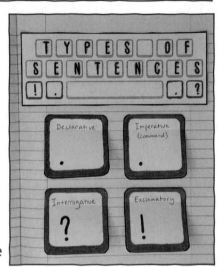

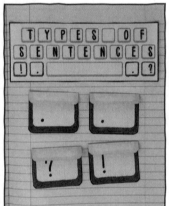
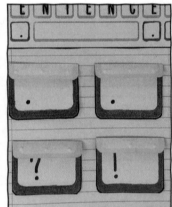

Procedures (Activity 2)

This short paragraph is meant to provide students with a few examples. I do it with my students rather than as independent practice.

1. Assign each type of sentence a color. Have students color code each sentence using the key. Add the correct punctuation mark to each line.
2. Check students' work for accuracy before cutting it out and gluing it into the notebook. I like to glue these examples on the left side of the page, opposite the templates from Activity 1.

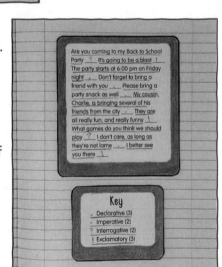

Notes for Template

declarative – makes a statement; punctuated with a period (ex. We take a spelling test on Friday.)

imperative – makes a command or polite request; punctuated with a period or exclamation mark (ex. Write your name at the top of the paper.)

exclamatory – expresses great emotion or excitement; punctuated with an exclamation mark (ex. I forgot to study last night!)

interrogative – asks a question; punctuated with a question mark (ex. What happens if I fail this test?)

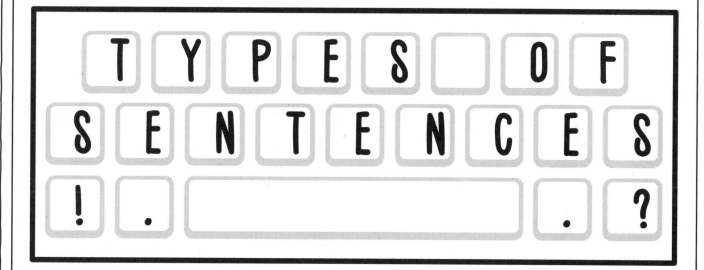

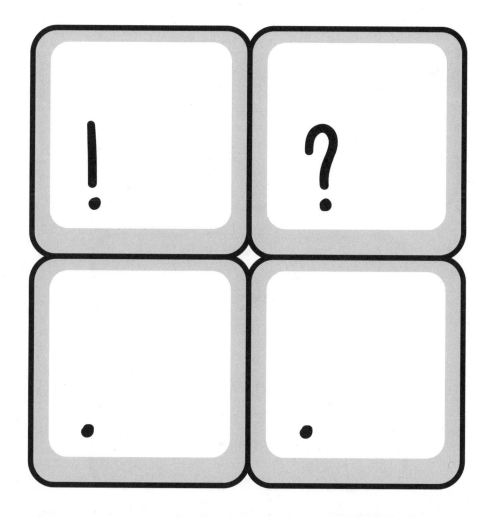

Are you coming to my Back to School Party _____ It's going to be a blast _____ The party starts at 6:00 pm on Friday night _____ Don't forget to bring a friend with you _____ Please bring a party snack as well _____ My cousin, Charlie, is bringing several of his friends from the city _____ They are all really fun, and really funny _____ What games do you think we should play _____ I don't care, as long as they're not lame _____ I better see you there _____

Key

Declarative (3)
Imperative (2)
Interrogative (2)
Exclamatory (3)

INTERACTIVE GRAMMAR NOTEBOOK
Lesson 2-2: Subject & Predicate

Purpose: Identify the simple subject and simple predicate of a sentence. Identify the complete subject and complete predicate of a sentence.

Procedures (Activity 1)

1. This is a simple matchbook fold. Cut out all three pieces, and then fold the top of the matchbook down flush with the top of the sentence section.
2. Glue the subject and predicate graphics onto the blank sides of the flaps. I like consistency and use red for nouns or subjects and purple for predicates or verbs.
3. Write the notes under the flaps. Refer to the Notes for Template section.
4. I underline the complete subject and box the simple subject. I did the same with the predicate. This will be continued throughout this lesson.

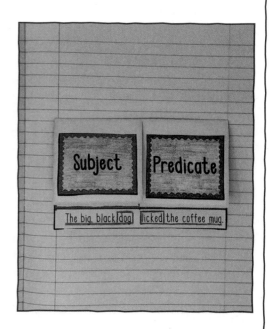

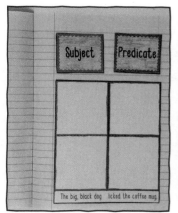
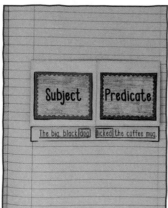
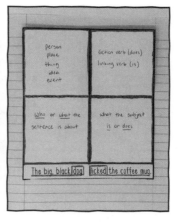

Notes for Template

subject – who or what the sentence is about; person, place, thing, idea, or event
predicate – what the subject is or does; action verb (does) or linking verb (is)

Procedures (Activity 2)

1. For this lesson, students will separate subjects and predicates in sentences, pull out simple subjects and complete predicates, and then make new sentences with the same simple subjects and simple predicates. But first, they will take some more in-depth notes on the topic.
2. Have students glue the *complete subject, simple subject, complete predicate,* and *simple predicate* pieces on the left-hand page. Write notes about each type on the page beside the piece. Refer to the Notes for Template section.
3. Complete the template with the sentences. In each sentence, underline the complete subject in red and the complete predicate in purple. Then, box the simple subject in red and the simple predicate in purple.
4. Cut out and glue the template with the sentences to the right-hand page opposite the notes page. Color and cut out the two blank templates (left side red, right side purple).
5. Next, use the blank template with the polka dots. Place small glue dots only in the indicated sections on the sides of the sentences template from step 3. Glue the polka dots template on top of the sentences template so that only the sides are glued down and the middle is free.

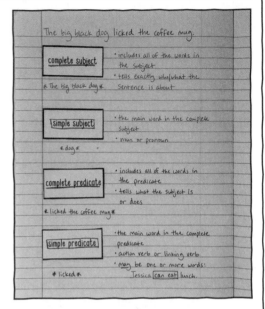

(Completed left-hand page)

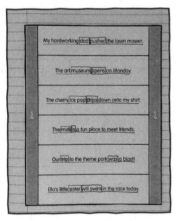

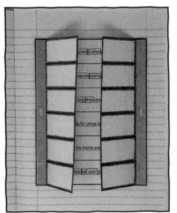
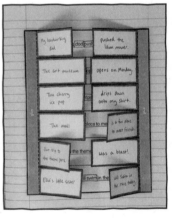

Notes for Template

complete subject – includes all of the words in the subject; tells exactly who/what the sentence is about (ex. The big, black dog)

simple subject – the main word in the complete subject; noun or pronoun (ex. dog)

complete predicate – includes all of the words in the predicate; tells what the subject is or does (ex. licked the coffee mug)

simple predicate – the main word in the complete predicate; action verb or linking verb; may be one or more words (ex: licked)

6. Snip the solid vertical line between the red and purple boxes.
7. On the left side, write each complete subject. Do the same on the right for the complete predicates. Then, snip each solid horizontal line.
8. Finally, use the blank template with the zigzags. Glue it on top of the polka dot template so that only the sides are glued down and the middle is free.
9. Repeat steps 6 and 7 with the zigzag-accented layer. This time, write only the simple subject and simple predicate.
10. Finally, I have students use a tablet-sized, lined sticky note and make up new sentences for the same simple subjects and simple predicates. I place the sticky note under both sets of flaps when finished.
11. Consider reinforcing this page with a paper clip. Or, place a lift-up tab under the activity to keep the page together.

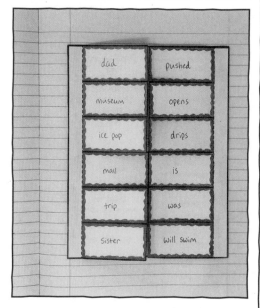

(Completed right-hand page)

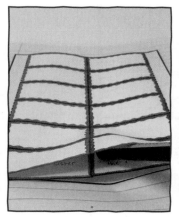
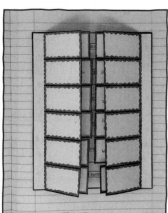
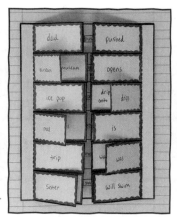

The big, black dog | licked the coffee mug.

Subject | Predicate

INTERACTIVE GRAMMAR NOTEBOOK
Lesson 2-2: Subject & Predicate

My hardworking dad pushed the lawn mower.

The art museum opens on Monday.

The cherry ice pop drips down onto my shirt.

The mall is a fun place to meet friends.

Our trip to the theme park was a blast!

Ella's little sister will swim in the race today.

glue

glue

imlovinlit.com

complete subject	complete predicate

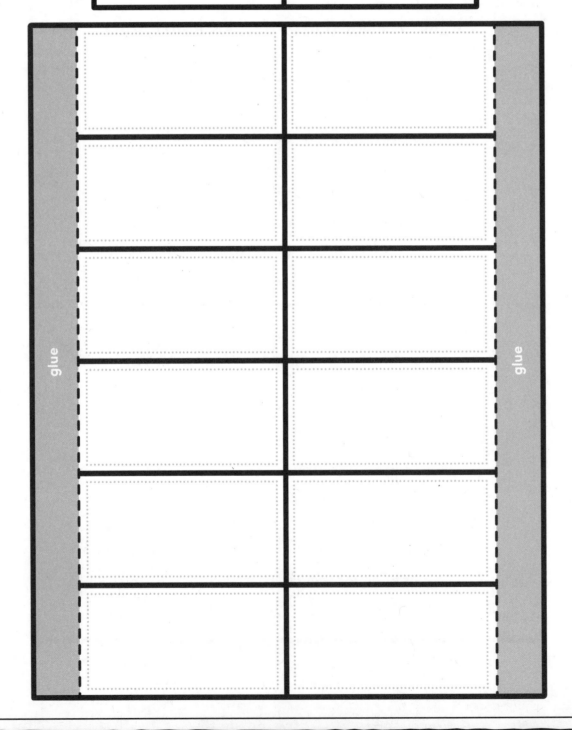

INTERACTIVE GRAMMAR NOTEBOOK
Lesson 2-2: Subject & Predicate

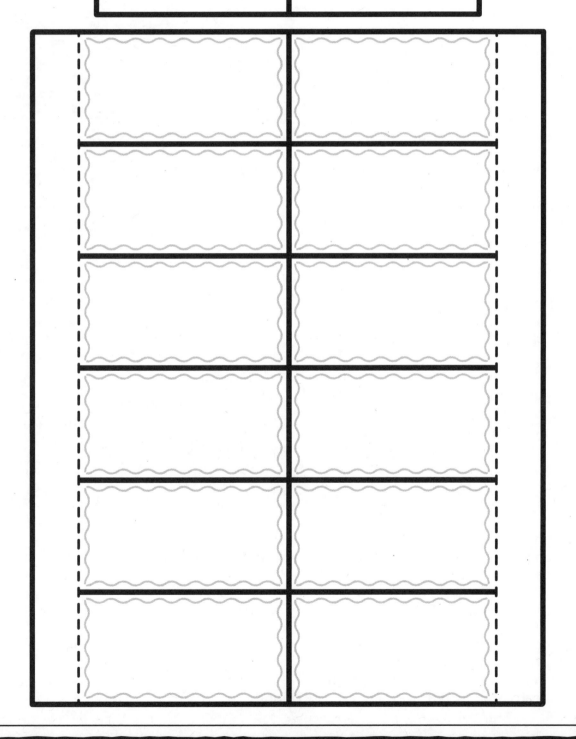

simple subject	simple predicate

INTERACTIVE GRAMMAR NOTEBOOK
Lesson 2-3: Compound Subjects & Compound Predicates

Purpose: Recognize and identify sentences with compound subjects and compound predicates. Add subjects and predicates to sentences to make compound subjects and compound predicates.

Procedures

1. Outline the subject pieces in red and the predicate pieces in purple. On the model sentence, box the word *Tori* in red, box *reads* in purple, and underline *reads nightly* in purple.
2. Cut out all of the pieces. Glue the title and model sentence to the top of the page, or across the long side of the page.
3. Stack the pieces to make two four-flap booklets. Glue the largest piece down. Then, placing glue only on the tabs, glue the next three pieces on top.
4. Write the definition on the top tab. Then, build the model sentence by adding the subject and predicates indicated. Refer to the Notes for Template section.

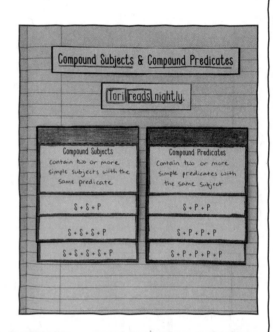

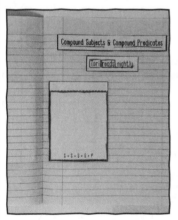 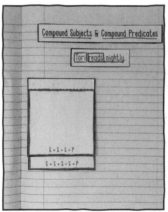 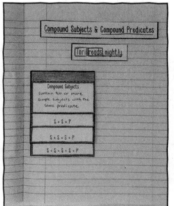 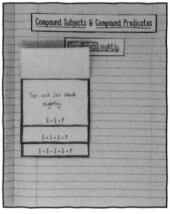

Notes for Template

Top tab: Compound Subjects – contain two or more simple subjects with the same predicate
2nd tab: Tori and Jen read nightly.
3rd tab: Tori, Jen, and Randy read nightly.
4th tab: Tori, Jen, Randy, and Brad read nightly.

Top Tab: Compound Predicates – contain two or more simple predicates that have the same subject
2nd tab: Tory reads and studies nightly.
3rd tab: Tory reads, studies, and practices nightly.
4th tab: Tori reads, studies, practices, and exercises nightly.

Compound Subjects

S + S + P

S + S + S + S + P

S + S + S + P

Compound Subjects & Compound Predicates

Tori reads nightly.

Compound Predicates

S + P + P

S + P + P + P + P

S + P + P + P

INTERACTIVE GRAMMAR NOTEBOOK
Lesson 2-4: Simple & Compound Sentences

Purpose: Distinguish between simple sentences and compound sentences. Join two simple sentences with a comma and a conjunction or a semicolon.

Procedures

1. For this lesson, you will be "building" double cookie sandwiches to show how two sentences can be stuck together with conjunctions (icing). Reference the unit on coordinating conjunctions later in this book (page 91).
2. Cut out all of the pieces. Write *(conjunction)* on the icing jar. Then, write the seven coordinating conjunctions around the icing jar: *and, but, for, nor, or, so,* and *yet.* Glue it to the page.
3. Build the explanation cookie. Glue the *Simple Sentence 1*, *comma + conjunction OR semicolon*, and *Simple Sentence 2* pieces together to form a cookie with icing in the middle.
4. Glue all of the cookies to the page. In the middle section (icing), write a conjunction or use a semicolon to complete the sandwiches. Add any missing punctuation to the sentences.
5. Bring this lesson to life for your students by bringing in chocolate chip cookies and white icing to make double cookie sandwiches. They'll never forget that a compound sentence consists of two simple sentences (cookies) joined with a conjunction (icing)!

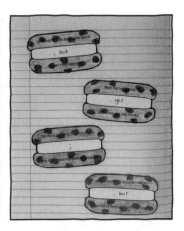

INTERACTIVE GRAMMAR NOTEBOOK
Lesson 2-4: Simple & Compound Sentences

Amy read a book about outer space

it wasn't very interesting

Mars has two moons

Saturn has over sixty moons

Simple Sentence 2

comma + conjunction OR semicolon

Simple Sentence 1

ICING

A spacesuit costs about $11 million

over half of the cost is for the backpack

The moon is drifting away from Earth

it only drifts about four centimeters per year

©2018 Erin Cobb • CD-105004

INTERACTIVE GRAMMAR NOTEBOOK
Lesson 2-5: Independent & Dependent Clauses

Purpose: Distinguish between independent and dependent clauses. Identify subordinating conjunctions used to add dependent clauses to independent clauses. Practice adding relevant dependent clauses to independent clauses.

Procedures (Activity 1)

1. Cut out the first template (page 41).
2. Fold the template on the dashed lines as shown. Note that the *subordinating conjunction* tab is folded inward under the *dependent clauses* tab.
3. Flip the template over. It should look like the second photo.
4. Write notes on the template. Refer to the Notes for Template section on page 40. Note that you are writing notes on top of the tabs, between the tabs, and under the tabs.
5. Glue the back of the template to the right-hand page.

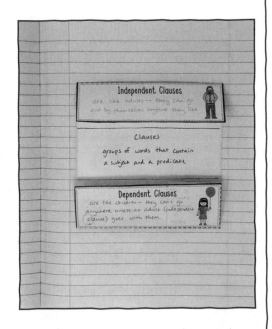

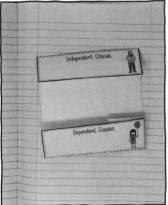

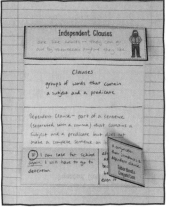

INTERACTIVE GRAMMAR NOTEBOOK
Lesson 2-5: Independent & Dependent Clauses

Procedures (Activity 2)

1. I like to glue in this template (page 42) on the left-hand page, opposite the page that contains Activity 1.
2. Each of these phrases is an independent clause, so outline in blue the prewritten clauses.
3. Write a dependent clause to go with each independent clause. Use editing marks to make any necessary changes. Use the list of subordinating conjunctions to help you. Then, outline in pink the dependent clauses. I also like to circle in purple the coordinating conjunctions.
4. Cut the table out and fold it inward on the dashed line. Glue the left side down so the right side swings open to the right.

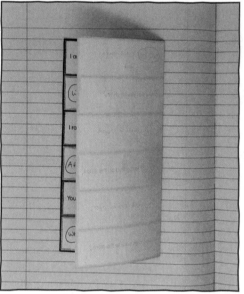

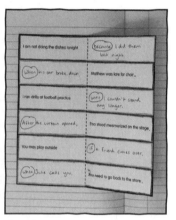

Notes for Template

Independent Clauses

(On flap) are like adults—they can go out by themselves any time they like

(Back of flap) independent clause – part of a sentence (separated with a comma) that makes a complete sentence on its own

(Under flap) If I am late for school again, I will have to go to detention. (Circle and label the independent clause *I will have to go to detention*.)

Clauses – groups of words that contain a subject and a predicate

Dependent Clauses

(On flap) are like children—they can't go anywhere unless an adult (independent clause) goes with them

(Back of flap) If I am late for school again, I will have to go to detention. (Circle and label the dependent clause *If I am late for school again,*.)

(Under flap) dependent clause – part of a sentence (separated with a comma) that contains a subject and a predicate but does not make a complete sentence on its own

Subordinate Conjunction

(On flap) a conjunction that introduces a dependent clause

(Under flap) after, as, because, before, even if, if, once, since, so that, than, that, though, unless, until, when, where, whereas, whether, while, why

Dependent Clauses

Subordinate
Conjunction

Independent Clauses

I am not doing the dishes tonight	
	Matthew was late for choir
I ran drills at football practice	
	Elsa stood mesmerized on the stage
You may play outside	
	You need to go back to the store

INTERACTIVE GRAMMAR NOTEBOOK
Lesson 2-6: Sentences, Fragments, & Run-Ons

Purpose: Identify sentences, fragments, and run-ons. Correct fragments and run-ons to make complete sentences.

Procedures

1. Cut out the entire template and fold it on the dashed line.
2. Next, write the notes for each word on top of the tab to the right of the word. Refer to the Notes for Template section.
3. Glue the back of the left side of the template only (the section with *Sentence, Fragment,* and *Run-On*) so the tabs on the right swing open.
4. Cut the solid lines between the right-hand tabs.
5. Write an example under each tab. Refer to the Notes for Template section.

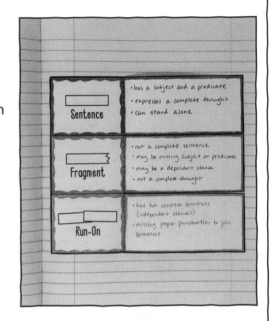

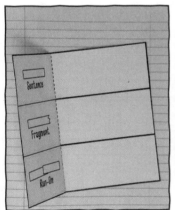 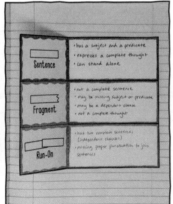 

Notes for Template

sentence – (top of tab) has a subject and a predicate; expresses a complete thought; can stand alone; (under tab) Mary plays the guitar well.

fragment – (top of tab) not a complete sentence; may be missing subject or predicate; may be a dependent clause; not a complete thought; (under tab) Plays the guitar well. OR Because Mary plays the guitar well.

run-on – (top of tab) has two complete sentences (independent clauses); missing proper punctuation to join sentences; (under tab) Mary plays the guitar well she won an award.

INTERACTIVE GRAMMAR NOTEBOOK
Lesson 2-6: Sentences, Fragments, & Run-Ons

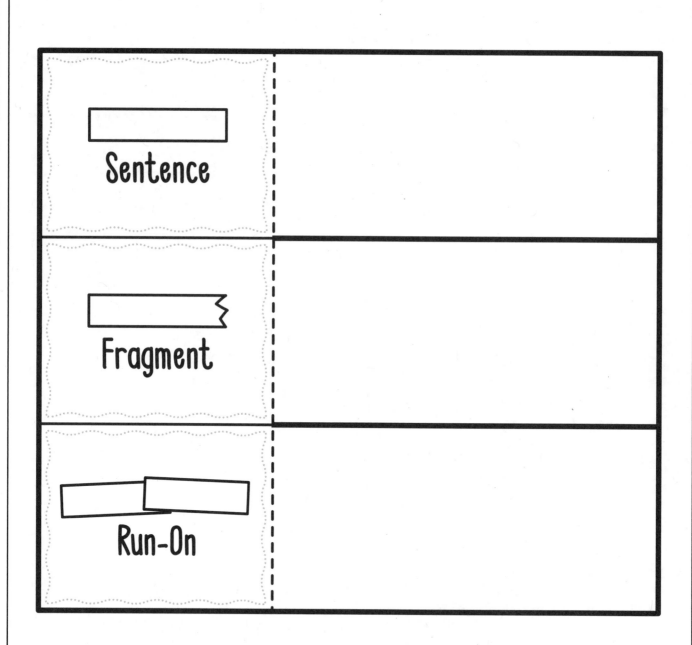

Sentence

Fragment

Run-On

INTERACTIVE GRAMMAR NOTEBOOK
Lesson 3-1: Common & Proper Nouns

Purpose: Distinguish between common and proper nouns. Change nouns from proper to common and from common to proper.

Procedures

1. To distinguish between common and proper nouns, I have removed the faces and the book's title on the *Common Nouns* tab. This is to represent any boy, girl, or book, not specific ones. When we see their faces or the title, we will name them using proper nouns.
2. Cut out all of the pieces of the template.
3. Fold back the tabs on the top flaps. Place glue on the backs of the tabs only so the tabs swing open from the top.
4. At the bottom of the page, glue the left and right tabs only. Do not glue the portion with words on it.
5. Allow it to dry for one minute. Then, cut the solid vertical line in the middle of the template to separate the sides.
6. Write the notes for each type of noun under the tabs. Refer to the Notes for Template section.
7. Now, snip each solid horizontal line between the words so that each tab swings open freely.
8. Finally, write the opposite type of noun under each tab. If the tab says, "University Boulevard," that's a proper noun, so write a related common noun for that proper noun under the tab, such as "street" or "boulevard." Under the "waitress" tab, you might write "Susan" or "Mrs. Brown."
9. Remember that for a noun to be a proper noun, *it must be a name that was given to it by a person or people.*

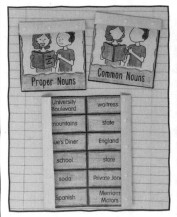

Notes for Template

proper nouns – special names for nouns; always begin with a capital letter; names that have been given to people, places, or things

common nouns – general names for non-specific nouns; words that should be found in the dictionary; do not begin with capital letters

Proper Nouns

Common Nouns

University Boulevard	waitress
mountains	state
Sue's Diner	England
school	store
soda	Private Jones
Spanish	Merriam Motors

INTERACTIVE GRAMMAR NOTEBOOK
Lesson 3-2: Concrete & Abstract Nouns

Purpose: Distinguish between concrete and abstract nouns. Identify a noun as being concrete or abstract and explain why.

Procedures

1. This page is very similar to the previous lesson. Notice that I used a lot of red in both lessons—since red is my color for subjects and nouns, I decided to stick with it for both of these templates.
2. Start by cutting out all of the pieces. Just like in the previous lesson, fold back the top tabs for the concrete nouns and abstract nouns pieces and glue just the tabs at the top of the page.
3. Write the definition for each type of noun under the tab. See the Notes for Template section.
4. I recommend filling out the bottom chart before gluing it to the page below the tabs and definitions.

Notes for Template

concrete nouns – "regular" nouns (the kind you learned about in first grade); can be experienced with the five senses (touch, sight, taste, smell, hearing)

abstract nouns – ideas or concepts; cannot be detected or experienced with the five senses

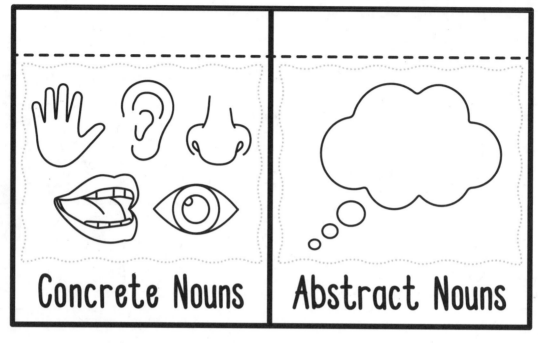

Concrete Nouns   Abstract Nouns

Noun	Concrete or Abstract?	Prove It
pizza	concrete	I can smell, taste, see, and feel pizza.
freedom		
puppy		
luck		
October		
Mrs. Gilbert		

Purpose: Distinguish between singular and plural nouns. Identify specific rules for making singular words plural. Make singular nouns plural by following rules.

Procedures (Activity 1)

1. This lesson is a more visual and simple version of the "Hard & Fast Rules for Using Plurals" in Unit 1 (page 20). They can be used interchangeably, or you might choose to only use one or the other.
2. Start by coloring each section of the template (page 50) a different color. Cut out the entire *S*. Then, cut apart the *S* by cutting on the solid lines.
3. Fold up each tab. As usual, you are going to glue the back of the tab only.
4. Glue down the tabs so that together they form the *S*.
5. Write the rules for each condition under the tab. Refer to the Notes for Template section.

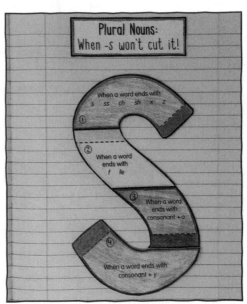

Procedures (Activity 2)

1. Activity 2 is simply a chart (page 51) to be completed to practice using these rules. You can use Activity 2 along with the *S* template, or with the "Hard & Fast Rules" practice sheet (page 21) if you prefer.
2. Before completing the chart, have students number each tab in the *S* from top to bottom.
3. To complete the activity, students simply make each noun in the left column plural and then indicate which rule was used. I like to force my students to provide the rule number to make sure that my good spellers aren't just going with their instincts.
4. I glue this page on the left-hand side of the page, opposite the *S* template. Or, glue it with the "Hard & Fast Rules" if you used those instead.

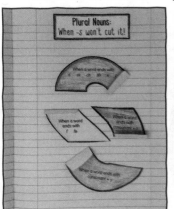  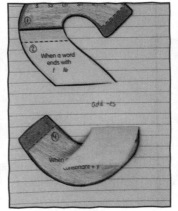 

Notes for Template

s, ss, ch, sh, x, or z – add -*es*, like in *buses*

f or fe – change *f* to *v* and add -*es*, like in *knives*

consonant + *o* – add -*es*

consonant + *y* – change *y* to *i* and add -*es*, as in *babies*

Plural Nouns:
When -s won't cut it!

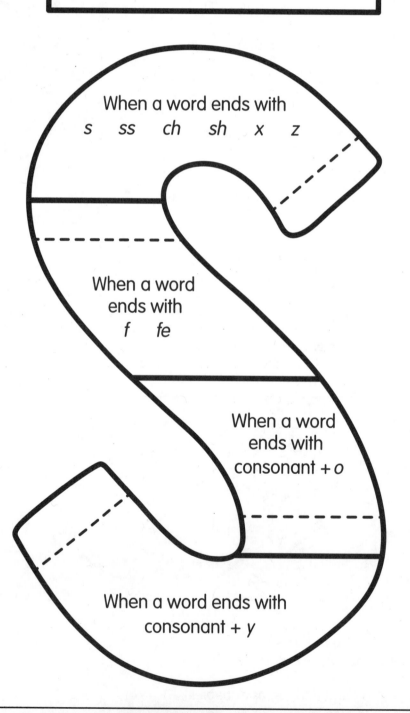

When a word ends with
s   ss   ch   sh   x   z

When a word
ends with
f   fe

When a word
ends with
consonant + *o*

When a word ends with
consonant + *y*

INTERACTIVE GRAMMAR NOTEBOOK
Lesson 3-3: Plural Nouns

Singular	Plural	Rule #
dish		
hero		
country		
goddess		
shelf		
life		
watch		
tragedy		
echo		
society		
glass		

INTERACTIVE GRAMMAR NOTEBOOK
Lesson 3-4: Possessive Nouns

Purpose: Identify possessive nouns. Follow standard rules to make nouns possessive.

Procedures

1. In the case of making Arkansas possessive (or another noun that ends with a silent *s*), I have my students add *'s* for the sake of consistency, even though just an apostrophe is correct as well. I do point out that both options are correct, though.
2. To make the template, start by cutting out the entire thing.
3. Then, snip the horizontal lines under *most nouns* and *two nouns share* to separate those two tabs.
4. Now, snip the horizontal lines above the three conditions for plural nouns to separate those three tabs as well.
5. Fold each of the tabs up so that you can put glue only in the middle (behind *Possessive Nouns*), top (behind *Singular*), and bottom (behind *Plural*) sections.
6. Now that you've glued down the part shown in red, write the notes for each condition under the tab. Refer to the Notes for Template section.

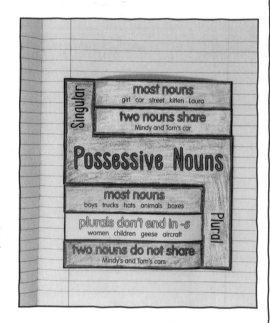

   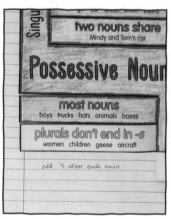

Notes for Template

Singular

most nouns – add *'s*, even if the singular noun ends with an *s*, such as in *Arkansas* or *James*

two nouns share – add an *'s* after the second noun only if they share one thing

Plural

most nouns – add an apostrophe after the existing *s* to make boys', trucks', etc.

plurals that don't end in -s – add *'s*

two nouns that do not share – add *'s* after each noun

INTERACTIVE GRAMMAR NOTEBOOK
Lesson 3-4: Possessive Nouns

Singular

most nouns
girl   car   street   kitten   Laura

two nouns share
Mindy and Tom's car

Possessive Nouns

most nouns
boys   trucks   hats   animals   boxes

plurals don't end in -s
women   children   geese   aircraft

Plural

two nouns do not share
Mindy's and Tom's cars

INTERACTIVE GRAMMAR NOTEBOOK
Lesson 4-1: Action, Linking, & Helping Verbs

Purpose: Identify, define, and provide examples for the three types of verbs: action verbs, linking verbs, and helping verbs.

Procedures

1. Color and cut out the template.
2. Flip it to the back and fold the tabs toward the middle as shown.
3. Write a description for each verb type under the appropriate tab. Include the examples as well. Refer to the Notes for Template section.
4. Either glue the provided lists of common helping and linking verbs (page 56) on the left-hand page opposite this activity, or have students write the lists out in that space themselves. Note that some are both helping and linking verbs; discuss why this is.

Notes for Template

action verbs – words that express action (ex. Joey <u>runs</u> in the race.)

linking verbs – words that show a state of being (ex. Joey <u>is</u> the fastest runner.)

helping verbs – words that help the main verb express an action or state of being; helping verbs are part of a verb phrase that includes the helping verb and an action or linking verb (ex. Joey <u>might</u> win the race.)

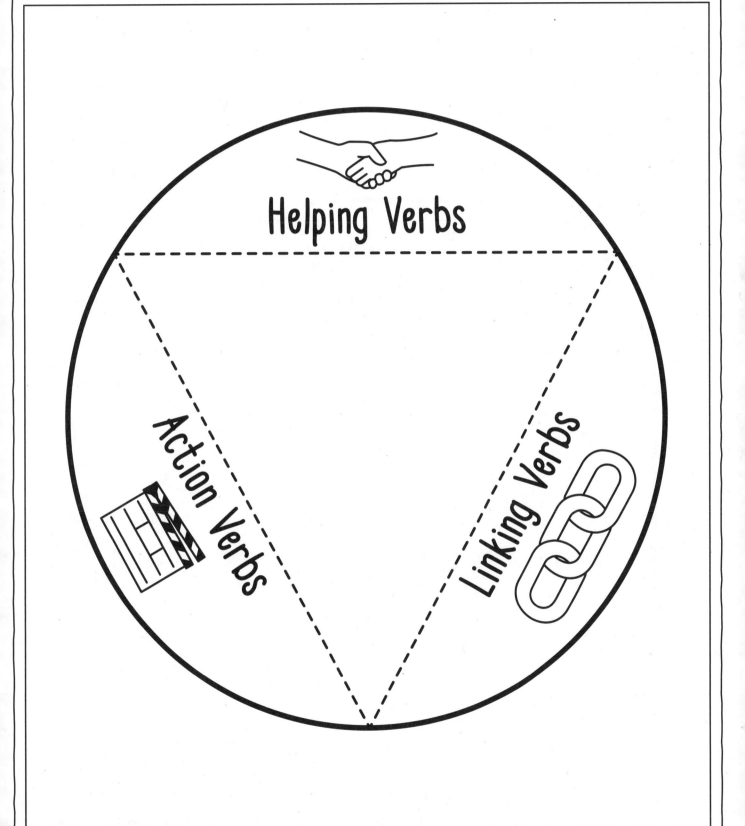

INTERACTIVE GRAMMAR NOTEBOOK
Lesson 4-1: Action, Linking, & Helping Verbs

Common Linking Verbs 		Common Helping Verbs 		
am	appear	am	have	may
are	become	are	has	might
is	feel	is	had	must
was	grow	was	can	shall
were	sound	were	could	should
be	seem	be	do	will
being	look	being	does	would
been	taste	been	did	

INTERACTIVE GRAMMAR NOTEBOOK
Lesson 4-2: Predicate Nominatives & Predicate Adjectives

Purpose: Identify and distinguish between predicate nominatives and predicate adjectives. Describe the function of each.

Procedures

1. I like to start this lesson by telling students that predicate nominatives and predicate adjectives sound very complicated, but they are so simple! Be sure to connect this lesson with the previous lesson, specifically linking verbs.
2. Cut out the two pieces. For the predicate nominative, write the sentence, "Sam is a doctor." inside the links as shown. Then, in the predicate adjective piece, write "I was tired."
3. Glue down the tabs for each piece. Then, snip the vertical lines between the links.
4. Write the definitions for predicate nominatives and predicate adjectives above each tab-template, as shown.
5. Read the sorting sentences. Decide which sentences have predicate nominatives and which have predicate adjectives. Then, write each part of each sentence under the correct tab. Refer to the Notes for Template section.

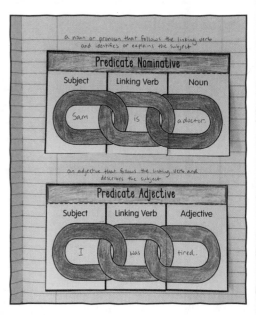

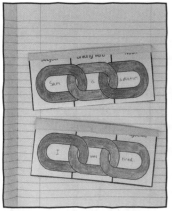 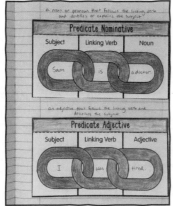 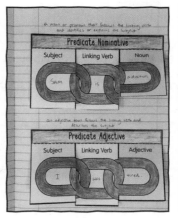 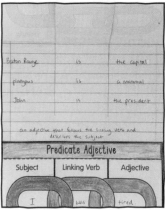

Notes for Template

predicate nominative – a noun or pronoun that follows the linking verb and identifies or explains the subject

predicate adjective – an adjective that follows the linking verb and describes the subject

Sorting Sentences*
1. My headache / became / worse. (adjective)
2. Charlie / seems / upset ~~about his grades~~. (adjective)
3. Baton Rouge / is / the capital ~~of Louisiana~~. (nominative)
4. The platypus / is / a mammal. (nominative)
5. This job / seems / difficult. (adjective)
6. John / is / the president ~~of Student Council~~. (nominative)

*Notice that I did not include the prepositional phrases under the tabs, as they are extra information and there is only room for the basic subject-predicate structures that are being emphasized here.

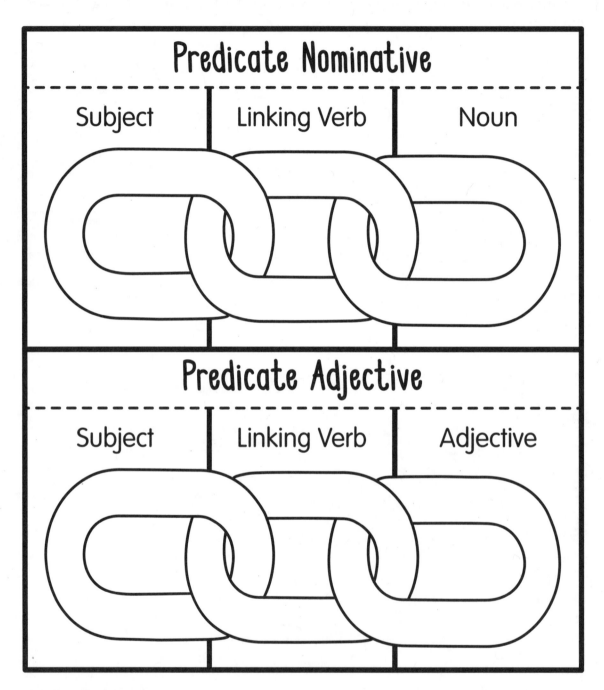

Predicate Nominative

| Subject | Linking Verb | Noun |

Predicate Adjective

| Subject | Linking Verb | Adjective |

Sorting Sentences

1. My headache became worse.

2. Charlie seems upset about his grades.

3. Baton Rouge is the capital of Louisiana.

4. The platypus is a mammal.

5. This job seems difficult.

6. John is the president of Student Council.

INTERACTIVE GRAMMAR NOTEBOOK
Lesson 4-3: The Perfect Tense Fence

Purpose: Identify and distinguish between these tenses: past, present, future, past perfect, present perfect, and future perfect. Classify sentences according to their tense.

Procedures

1. Walk students through writing the information about each tense on its fence. Refer to the Notes for Template section.
2. Then, color the fences (no certain color) and cut them out.
3. Glue the fences onto a two-page spread in the notebook. Note: these fences make pockets! Be careful that you glue them down the correct way. Put glue dots on the sides and bottoms only so that the middle and top parts of the fences are open to form pockets that will accept the sentence strips. Place the glue dots close together so that the sentence strips will not fall out of the bottom. Also, make sure that the top fences are not so close to the top of the notebook that the sentences will stick out of the top of the notebook.
4. Cut out the sorting sentences and sort them into the correct fence pockets. Refer to the Notes for Template section for the answers.

  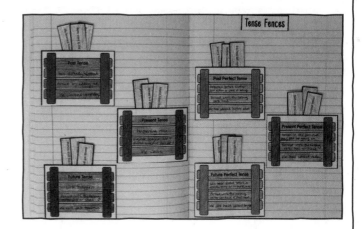

Notes for Template

present tense – happening now; singular subject: add -*s*, plural subject: do not add -*s* (ex: He walks.); sentences G, N, O

present perfect tense – began in the past and may still be going on; formed with the helping verbs *has* or *have* (ex. He has walked today.); sentences I, Q, R

past tense – has already happened; formed by adding -*ed* (ex. He walked yesterday.); sentences C, F, L

past perfect tense – happened before another past action or state of being; formed with the helping verb *had* (ex. He had walked before school.); sentences D, J, K

future tense – will happen; formed with the helping verbs *will* or *shall* (ex. He will walk tomorrow.); sentences A, H, P

future perfect tense – will have ended before a specific time or even in the future; formed with the helping verbs *will have* or *shall have* (ex. He will have walked tonight.); sentences B, E, M

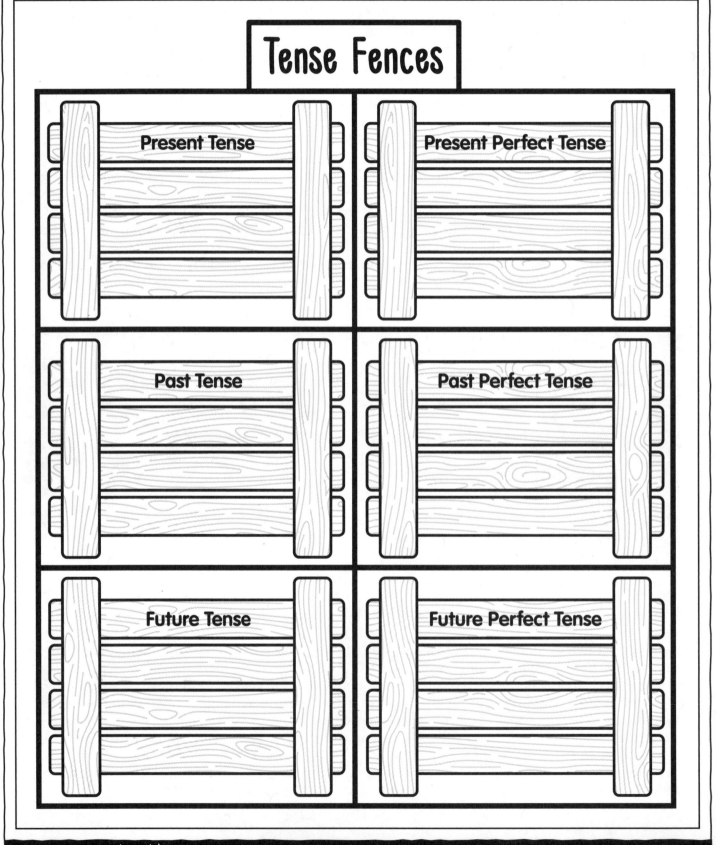

Tense Fences

Present Tense

Present Perfect Tense

Past Tense

Past Perfect Tense

Future Tense

Future Perfect Tense

INTERACTIVE GRAMMAR NOTEBOOK
Lesson 4-3: The Perfect Tense Fence

Mandy will go to the dentist on Friday. **A**	By the end of this month, the baby will have been born. **B**
Betty went to the museum when she was five. **C**	Erin had left early when she got stuck in traffic. **D**
Jay will have eaten dinner before the play. **E**	Grandfather wanted to get ice cream. **F**
James is a straight A student. **G**	The baby birds will eat when their mother returns. **H**
I have dreamed of becoming an astronaut. **I**	Jeremy had finished his algebra homework. **J**
Dr. Jones had assigned the take home test before Christmas break. **K**	We learned how to crochet at camp last week. **L**
The horse will have gotten dirty at the rodeo. **M**	Martin hikes through the forest to the pond. **N**
The girls swim in the river. **O**	Marcia shall buy two shirts and one pair of shorts. **P**
Julie has slept poorly every night this week. **Q**	Barbara and Caleb have borrowed from me before. **R**

INTERACTIVE GRAMMAR NOTEBOOK
Lesson 4-4: Infinitives & Participles (Principal Parts)

Purpose: Identify and distinguish between the four principal parts of verbs: infinitive, present participle, past, and past participle.

Procedures (Activity 1)

1. Begin with the ice pop template (page 63). Color if desired and cut out. (I don't have any special color-coding here.)
2. Crease the right side up toward the left. Open it back up and glue down the left side only (behind the ice pop).
3. Snip each horizontal line. Write each definition under the appropriate tab. Refer to the Notes for Template section.

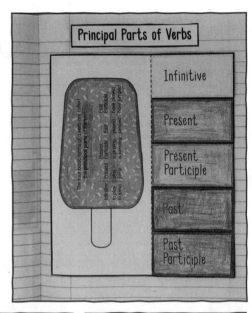

Procedures (Activity 2)

1. Cut out the three sentence strips (page 64).
2. Fold down the *(present participle)* tab and write the present participle on top (ex. am cooking) to make a new sentence.
3. Fold the *(past)* tab right. You'll need to include the subject on this strip since the tab covers it (ex. I cooked).
4. Fold up the *(past participle)* tab and write the past participle on top (ex. have cooked).

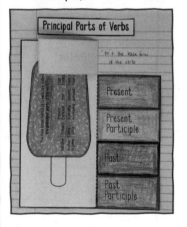

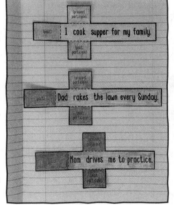

Procedures (Activity 3)

1. Use these charts (pages 65 and 66) to give students controlled practice in altering tenses and to provide a reference for irregular verb tenses. Simply cut out the tables, complete, check, and glue them into the notebook.

Notes for Template

infinitive – *to* + the base form of the verb
present – used to express a current action or state; use the infinitive without *to*
present participle – used to form continuous tense; formed by adding the helping verb *is* before the verb and adding *-ing* to the base form of the verb
past – used to express a previous action or a state that previously existed; add *-ed*
past participle – used to show that something started in the past but still continues; formed by adding the helping verb *have* before the verb and adding *-ed* to the base form of the verb

Principal Parts of Verbs

The four basic forms of a verb are called the **principal parts** of the verb.

Infinitive	Present	Present Participle	Past	Past Participle
to play	play	is playing	played	have played
to jump	jump	is jumping	jumped	have jumped

Infinitive

Present

Present Participle

Past

Past Participle

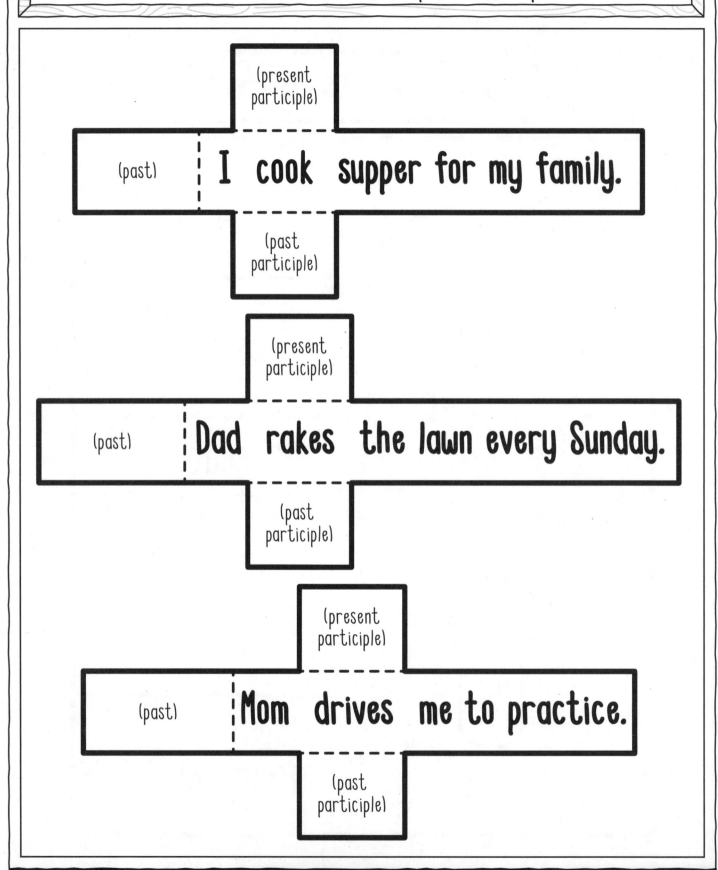

(present participle)

(past)   I cook supper for my family.

(past participle)

(present participle)

(past)   Dad rakes the lawn every Sunday.

(past participle)

(present participle)

(past)   Mom drives me to practice.

(past participle)

Common Irregular Verbs

Infinitive	Present	Present Participle	Past	Past Participle
to begin				
to blow				
to break				
to bring				
to build				
to choose				
to come				
to draw				
to drink				
to drive				
to eat				
to fall				
to fly				
to freeze				
to give				
to go				
to grow				
to hear				
to hold				
to know				

Common Irregular Verbs

Infinitive	Present	Present Participle	Past	Past Participle
to lead				
to lend				
to make				
to pay				
to ride				
to ring				
to run				
to see				
to shrink				
to sink				
to sing				
to speak				
to steal				
to swim				
to take				
to throw				
to win				
to write				

Purpose: Define and identify direct and indirect objects.

Procedures

1. Color the definition templates if desired and cut out all of the pieces.
2. I call these folds butterfly folds. Only the center area (colored red in the photo) is glued down, and the sides swing open from the middle. Crease each of the sides of the red area, then glue down the red area. It should resemble a butterfly on the page with the Direct and Indirect Objects tabs being the "wings."
3. Repeat for the sentence templates. Crease around the horizontal center tab, and then glue down the middle section (behind the sentences).
4. Snip the solid vertical lines so each side opens freely.
5. Write the definitions under the Direct and Indirect Objects tabs. Refer to the Notes for Template section.
6. For the sentence tabs, lift each question and write the object under the tab.

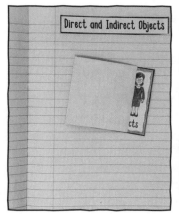

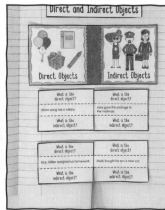

Notes for Template

direct objects – the receiver of the action; answers *Who?* or *What?*
indirect objects – someone or something affected by the action of the verb; answers *To whom?* or *For whom?*

Mom sang me a lullaby. DO: lullaby; IO: me
Joey gave the package to the mailman. DO: package; IO: mailman
Mrs. Miller assigned us homework. DO: homework; IO: us
Mark bought her son a new car. DO: car; IO: son

Direct and Indirect Objects

Direct Objects

Indirect Objects

What is the direct object?	What is the direct object?
Mom sang me a lullaby.	Joey gave the package to the mailman.
What is the indirect object?	What is the indirect object?

What is the direct object?	What is the direct object?
Mrs. Miller assigned us homework.	Mark bought his son a new car.
What is the indirect object?	What is the indirect object?

INTERACTIVE GRAMMAR NOTEBOOK
Lesson 5-1: Prepositions

Purpose: Identify prepositions and explain their purpose.

Procedures

1. Have students glue the *Prepositions* chart (page 71) into their notebooks for future reference.
2. The accordion fold template analyzes the main purposes of prepositions. As we construct the template, I have my students practice making prepositional phrases for each word to drill it into them.
3. Cut out the accordion template (page 70) in two pieces. Have students write in the prepositions for each purpose by looking at the *Prepositions* chart and trying to distinguish most of them themselves. Make sure they are writing accurate information since it will be a source of reference. Refer to the Notes for Template section.
4. After writing, coloring, and cutting out the pieces, place glue dots on the top of the tab next to the *How* section.
5. Glue the *Where* section on top of this tab to create a continuous chain. Then, crease the template accordion- or fan-style as shown.
6. Glue down the tab next to the title section.
7. Tuck the other folds under the title section. Use a scrap triangle as shown to keep it down. Be careful to only glue on the three points of the triangle to form a pocket, and hold it down as it dries (about one minute).

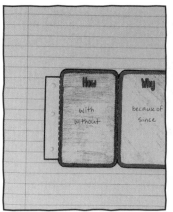
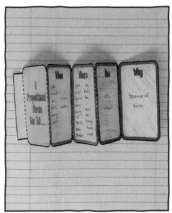

Notes for Template

when – after, around, at, before, during, past, since, until
where – above, across, against, along, among, at, behind, below, beneath, by, down, from, in, near, over, through, toward, under
how – with, without
why – because of, since

A
Prepositional
Phrase
Can Tell . . .

When

Where

How

Why

Prepositions

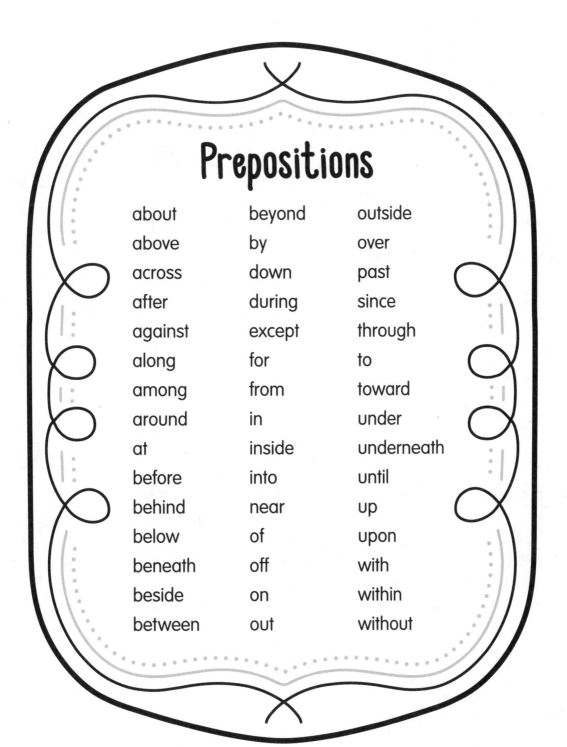

about	beyond	outside
above	by	over
across	down	past
after	during	since
against	except	through
along	for	to
among	from	toward
around	in	under
at	inside	underneath
before	into	until
behind	near	up
below	of	upon
beneath	off	with
beside	on	within
between	out	without

INTERACTIVE GRAMMAR NOTEBOOK
Lesson 5-2: Prepositional Phrases

Purpose: Recognize prepositional phrases. Complete prepositional phrases by adding a preposition or an object. Recognize the object of the preposition.

Procedures

1. This template includes two parts—a tab showing the relationship between prepositional phrases and the object of the preposition, and a short practice activity. Notice the coloring, which is important. The prepositional phrase piece is blue, while the object of the preposition is green. The object (shelf) is colored both colors to represent that it is both part of the prepositional phrase, but also the object of the preposition.
2. Color and cut out the pieces. Fold the tabs up or down and glue the pieces as shown so the pieces flip up and down.
3. Write the descriptions for each part under the appropriate tab. Refer to the Notes for Template section.
4. Complete the practice activity and glue it below the tab templates.

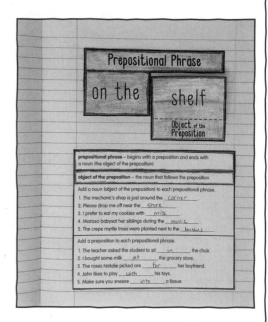

   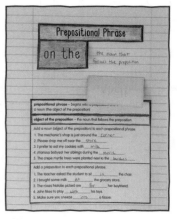

Notes for Template

prepositional phrase – begins with a preposition and ends with a noun (the object)
object of the preposition – the noun that follows the preposition

Prepositional Phrase

on the

shelf

Object of the Preposition

---

prepositional phrase – begins with a preposition and ends with a noun (the object of the preposition)

object of the preposition – the noun that follows the preposition

---

Add a noun (object of the preposition) to each prepositional phrase.

1. The mechanic's shop is just around the _____ .

2. Please drop me off near the _____ .

3. I prefer to eat my cookies with _____ .

4. Marissa babysat her siblings during the _____ .

5. The crepe myrtle trees were planted next to the _____ .

Add a preposition to each prepositional phrase.

1. The teacher asked the student to sit _____ the chair.

2. I bought some milk _____ the grocery store.

3. The roses Natalie picked are _____ her boyfriend.

4. John likes to play _____ his toys.

5. Make sure you sneeze _____ a tissue.

INTERACTIVE GRAMMAR NOTEBOOK
Lesson 5-3: Adverb Phrases & Adjective Phrases

Purpose: Identify the purpose of prepositional phrases and what they modify. Distinguish between adverb phrases and adjective phrases.

Procedures

1. Color and cut out the template as one piece.
2. Crease the template on the dashed line.
3. Glue down the side with the vertical writing, allowing the tabs on the right to swing open. Snip each horizontal line so that each part of speech tab opens freely.
4. Write an example sentence for each part of speech. Underline the phrase and draw an arrow to the word it modifies. Refer to the Notes for Template section.

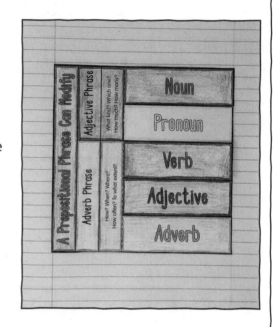

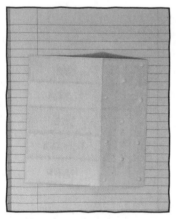 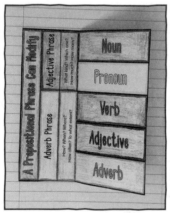 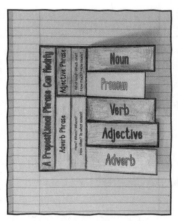 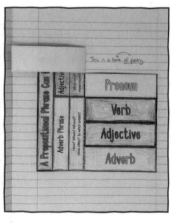

Notes for Template

noun – This is a book of poetry. (*of poetry* modifies *book*)
pronoun – The boss greeted everyone at the meeting. (*at the meeting* modifies *everyone*)
verb – She arrived in the morning. (*in the morning* modifies *arrived*)
adjective – Dad is happy with his new golf clubs. (*with his new golf clubs* modifies *happy*)
adverb – Keyon studies late at night. (*at night* modifies *late*)

A Prepositional Phrase Can Modify			
Adjective Phrase	What kind? Which one? How much? How many?	Noun	
		Pronoun	
Adverb Phrase	How? When? Where? How often? To what extent?	Verb	
		Adjective	
		Adverb	

noun – This is a book of poetry.

pronoun – The boss greeted everyone at the meeting.

verb – She arrived in the morning.

adjective – Dad is happy with his new golf clubs.

adverb – Keyon studies late at night.

imlovinlit.com

INTERACTIVE GRAMMAR NOTEBOOK
Lesson 6-1: Pronouns

Purpose: Identify pronouns and explain their purpose. Distinguish between the six types of pronouns: personal, possessive, indefinite, demonstrative, reflexive, and interrogative.

Procedures (Activity 1)

1. Color the *Types of Pronouns* template (page 78). It is not important which color you assign to each type of pronoun, but it is important that each one is a different color and consistent among your students.
2. Cut out the templates. Fold the top tabs back and glue behind the top tabs only. I like to put this page on the left-hand side of the notebook so that Activity 2 can be put on the right-hand side.
3. Snip on the solid lines to cut apart the tabs.
4. Lift up each tab and write a description for each pronoun type on the back of the tab. List the pronouns on the notebook paper under each tab. Refer to the Notes for Template section.

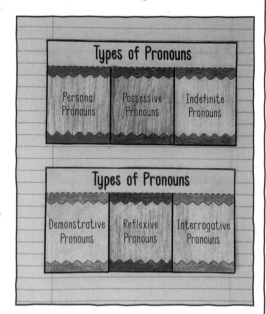

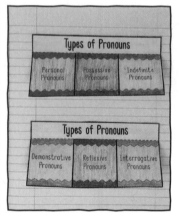
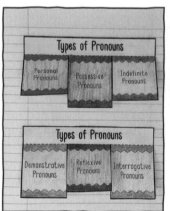
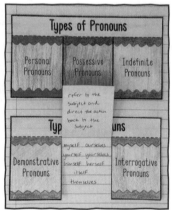

Notes for Template

personal pronouns – typical pronouns; replace the subject or object (ex. subjective: I, you, he, she, it, we, they; objective: me, you, him, her, it, us, them)

possessive pronouns – pronouns that show ownership (ex. my, you, his, hers, its, our, their, yours, ours, theirs)

indefinite pronouns – pronouns that do not refer to any specific person, amount, or thing (ex. anything, something, anyone, everyone, everybody, somebody, everything, nobody, no one, several, some, someone)

demonstrative pronouns – point out a specific person, place, thing, or idea (ex. this, that, these, those)

reflexive pronouns – refer to the subject and direct the action of the verb back to the subject (ex. myself, ourselves, yourself, yourselves, himself, herself, itself, themselves)

interrogative pronouns – pronouns that are used to ask questions and stand for something not yet known (ex. who, whom, whose, which, what)

INTERACTIVE GRAMMAR NOTEBOOK
Lesson 6-1: Pronouns

Procedures (Activity 2)

1. Do not start by coloring! Instead, cut out the template (page 79) as one piece and then work with it as described.
2. Read each sentence and identify the pronoun. Then, decide which type of pronoun it is. Circle the pronoun in the same color used for that type of pronoun in Activity 1. Then, outline the sentence's rectangle in that color. This color-coding will help students find examples of specific types in the future.
3. After circling and coloring, crease on the dashed line and glue the *Identifying Pronouns* tab down so that the sentences swing up freely.
4. Snip the solid lines between each sentence.
5. Now, go back and write the type of pronoun used in each sentence under its tab to reinforce the prounoun types again. Refer to the Notes for Template section.

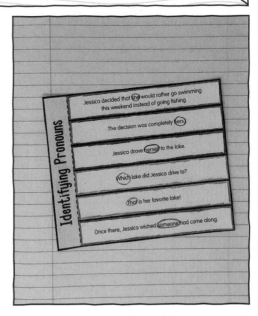

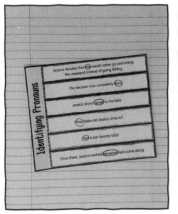 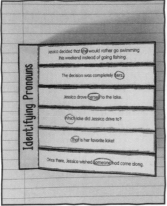 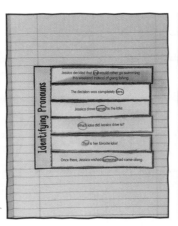 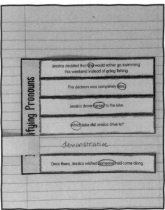

Notes for Template

Jessica decided that she would rather go swimming this weekend instead of going fishing. (*she*, personal pronoun)

The decision was completely hers. (*hers*, possessive pronoun)

Jessica drove herself to the lake. (*herself*, reflexive pronoun)

Which lake did Jessica drive to? (*which*, interrogative pronoun)

That is her favorite lake! (*that*, demonstrative pronoun)

Once there, Jessica wished someone had come along. (*someone*, indefinite pronoun)

Types of Pronouns

Personal Pronouns	Possessive Pronouns	Indefinite Pronouns

Types of Pronouns

Demonstrative Pronouns	Reflexive Pronouns	Interrogative Pronouns

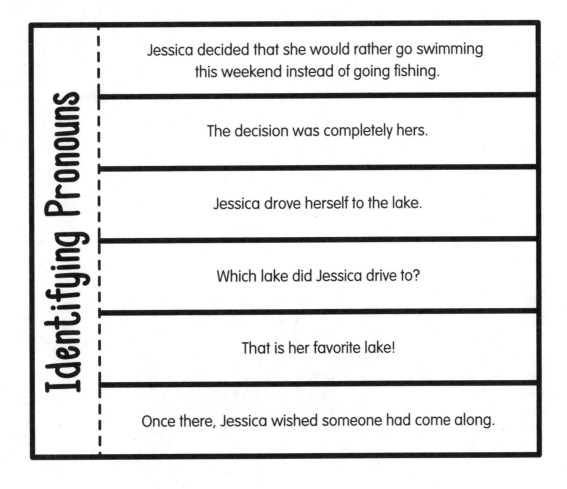

Identifying Pronouns

Jessica decided that she would rather go swimming this weekend instead of going fishing.

The decision was completely hers.

Jessica drove herself to the lake.

Which lake did Jessica drive to?

That is her favorite lake!

Once there, Jessica wished someone had come along.

INTERACTIVE GRAMMAR NOTEBOOK
Lesson 7-1: Kinds of Adjectives

Purpose: Identify four kinds of adjectives and their purposes.

Procedures

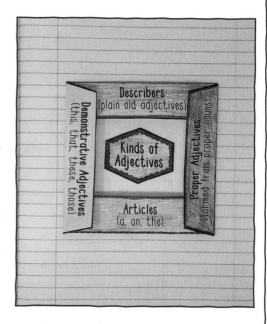

1. Cut out the template and color the tabs. Leave the middle section white, as this will be glued down in the notebook and will not show.
2. Flip the template over, and fold the tabs back so it looks like the photo below.
3. Glue the title (Kinds of Adjectives) into the blank white center.
4. Write the example sentences on the back sides of the appropriate tabs and circle all of the adjectives of that particular type in the sentence. Refer to the Notes for Template section. This is a good time to discuss the differences and similarities between demonstrative adjectives and demonstrative pronouns from lesson 6-1 (page 76).
5. Glue the blank white section down into the notebook.

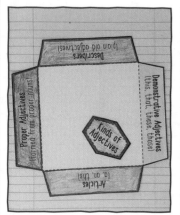 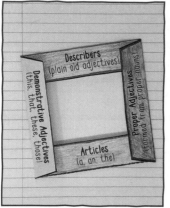 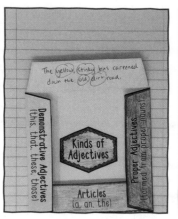 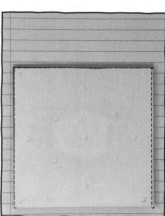

Notes for Template

describers – The yellow, stinky bus careened down the old dirt road. (yellow, stinky, old, dirt)
demonstrative adjectives – I prefer this brand of ice cream over that brand. (this, that)
proper adjectives – I like French bread for my sandwiches. (French)
articles – The volcano is a popular tourist attraction. (The, a)

Articles
(a, an, the)

Demonstrative Adjectives
(this, that, these, those)

Proper Adjectives
(formed from proper nouns)

Describers
(plain old adjectives)

Kinds of Adjectives

INTERACTIVE GRAMMAR NOTEBOOK
Lesson 7-2: Degrees of Comparison

Purpose: Identify the degrees of comparison. Change an adjective's degree. Explain the rules for changing degrees of comparison.

Procedures

1. Your students have no doubt been comparing by degrees for years, but mine typically have no idea about the syllable rules associated with deciding which form of the adjective is proper.
2. Color if desired (I stick with brown since these are adjectives) and cut out both templates. You're going to glue the smaller template on top of the larger one, allowing the degrees to swing up to reveal information.
3. Place glue dots on top of the *Degrees of Comparison* section of the larger template and glue the smaller template on top as shown.
4. Under the tabs, write the descriptions. Refer to the Notes for Template section.
5. As you complete the comparisons, discuss with students the rules as you write them at the bottom of the page. Refer to the Notes for Template section. Draw arrows to the relevant adjectives to emphasize the rules.

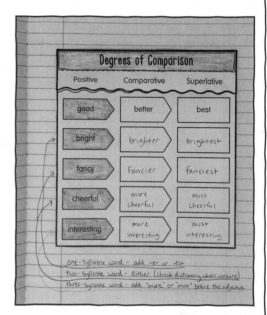

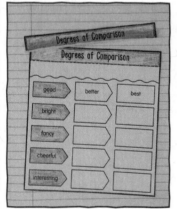
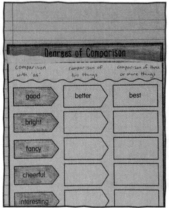
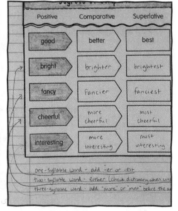

Notes for Template
positive – comparison with *as*
comparative – comparison of two things
superlative – comparison of three or more things

one-syllable word – add *-er* or *-est*
two-syllable word – either (check dictionary when unsure)
three-syllable word – add *more* or *most* before the adjective

Degrees of Comparison

good	better	best
bright		
fancy		
cheerful		
interesting		

Degrees of Comparison

Positive Comparative Superlative

INTERACTIVE GRAMMAR NOTEBOOK
Lesson 8-1: Adverbs

Purpose: Identify common adverbs and their purposes. Practice using different kinds of adverbs to describe an action.

Procedures

1. Color or outline the templates with color if desired and cut out the three plus sign-shaped templates.
2. Write in the sample words on the main adverbs template (page 85). Refer to the Notes for Template section.
3. Crease on the dashed lines and glue down only the middle section of the main template so all of the outer squares fold in to the center.
4. On the templates with the pictures (page 86), write a subject and a verb for the picture in the middle. Then, write an adverb in each square around it as appropriate. Refer to the Notes for Template section for examples.
5. Crease the two picture templates on the dashed lines and glue down the center sections as shown.
6. Write a sentence near each template using the various sentence parts on the template.

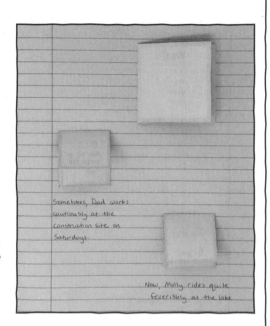

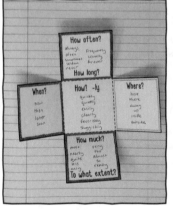 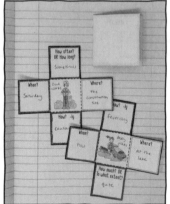 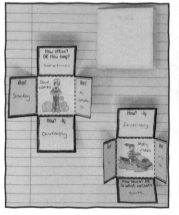 

Notes for Template

How often? How long? – always, often, sometimes, seldom, never, frequently, usually, forever
When? – now, then, later, soon
How? – quickly, quietly, easily, clearly, feverishly, sluggishly
Where? – here, there, away, up, inside, outside
How much? To what extent? – most, nearly, quite, less, only, very, too, almost, so, really

Construction worker (center, then clockwise from top) – Dad works; sometimes; the construction site; cautiously; Saturday; (ex. Sometimes, Dad works cautiously at the construction site on Saturdays.)
Jet ski rider (center, then clockwise from top) – Molly rides; feverishly; at the lake; quite; now (ex. Now, Molly rides quite feverishly at the lake.)

How often?

How long?

When?

How? -ly

Where?

How much?

To what extent?

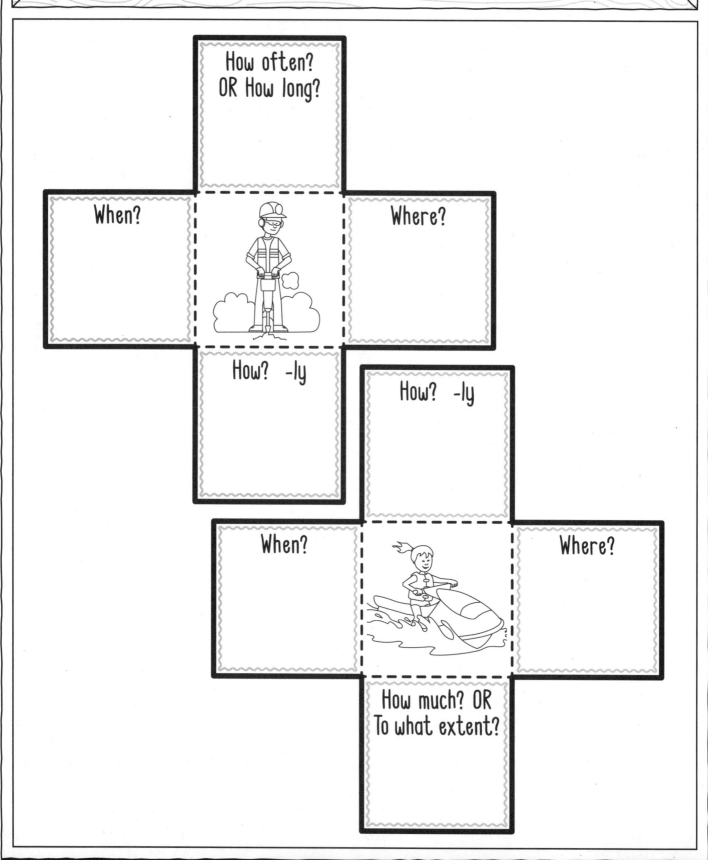

INTERACTIVE GRAMMAR NOTEBOOK
Lesson 8-2: More Adverb Phrases

Purpose: Identify and write adverb phrases that use *with*, *without*, and similes with *like* and *as*.

Procedures

1. The lesson adds to the previous adverb phrases lesson (lesson 5-3, page 74).
2. Color if desired and cut out the template. Fold it back and forth on the dashed lines like a fan or accordion.
3. Write an example sentence for each type of adverb phrase on the appropriate section. Underline the adverb phrase. Refer to the Notes for Template section for examples.
4. Glue down the title tab as well as the first *with* tab. The rest of the template will fold up to it.

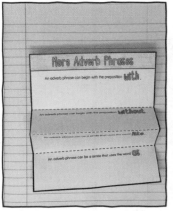
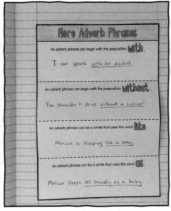

Notes for Template

with – I can speak <u>with an accent</u>.
without – You shouldn't drive <u>without a license</u>!
like – Marcus is sleeping <u>like a baby</u>.
as – Marcus sleeps <u>as soundly as a baby</u>.

More Adverb Phrases

An adverb phrase can begin with the preposition **with**.

An adverb phrase can begin with the preposition **without**.

An adverb phrase can be a simile that uses the word **like**.

An adverb phrase can be a simile that uses the word **as**.

INTERACTIVE GRAMMAR NOTEBOOK
Lesson 8-3: Double Negatives

Purpose: Recognize a double-negative error and correct it by eliminating a negative word.

Procedures

1. Color if desired and cut out the template.
2. Glue down the side and top only so that the sentence strips are not glued down.
3. Snip the solid lines so that the sentence strips swing open.
4. Read the sentences on the tabs. Cross out and/or change a negative word to correct the double negative. Then, write the corrected sentence under the tab.

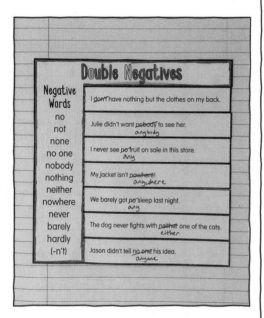

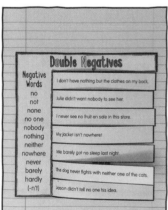
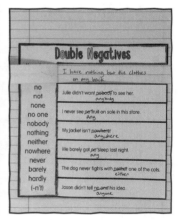

Double Negatives

Negative Words

no
not
none
no one
nobody
nothing
neither
nowhere
never
barely
hardly
(-n't)

I don't have nothing but the clothes on my back.
Julie didn't want nobody to see her.
I never see no fruit on sale in this store.
My jacket isn't nowhere!
We barely got no sleep last night.
The dog never fights with neither one of the cats.
Jason didn't tell no one his idea.

INTERACTIVE GRAMMAR NOTEBOOK
Lesson 9-1: Coordinating Conjunctions

Purpose: Identify and use coordinating conjunctions.

Procedures

1. Color and cut out the train template.
2. Write the coordinating conjunctions on the train. Write *Coordinating* on the left-hand tab, and *Conjunctions* on the train engine. Refer to the Notes for Template section for the conjunctions to write on each train car.
3. Put glue dots on the tab to the left of the second set of train cars. Place it behind the right-hand train on the first set to create one continuous train as shown.
4. Fold on the dashed lines like an accordion. For this one, I only folded every two train cars, but you could do it every train car if you prefer.
5. Glue down the left-hand tab only so that the rest of the train folds neatly under it.
6. Make a triangle holder to tuck the accordion fold into. See page 69, step 7 for more information on creating the pocket.
7. Write sentences using the conjunctions on the page below the train.

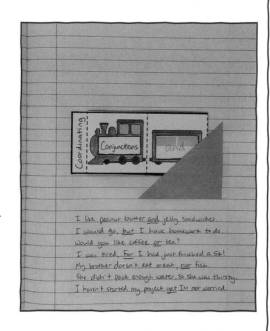

  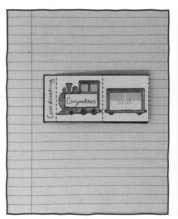 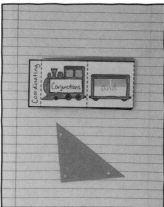

Notes for Template
and, but, or, for, nor, so, yet

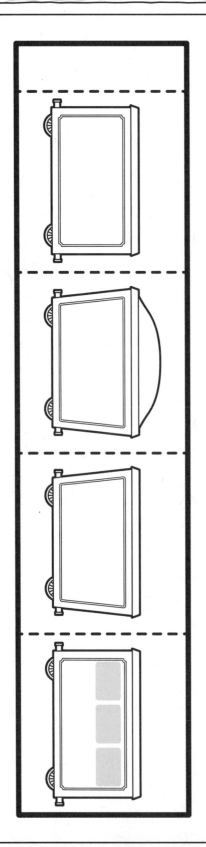
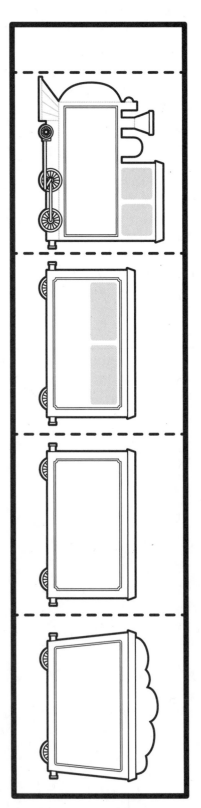

INTERACTIVE GRAMMAR NOTEBOOK
Lesson 9-2: Correlative Conjunctions

Purpose: Identify and use correlative conjunctions.

Procedures

1. Color and cut out the template. Any colors will work, as long as they are alternating as shown. Write each pair of coordinating conjunctions on the tabs.
2. Crease on the dashed lines and glue down the two side tabs only, leaving the middle word tabs free.
3. Cut the vertical solid line up the middle. Then, snip the horizonal solid lines.
4. Open each pair of correlative conjunction tabs and write a sample sentence for each conjunction pair under the tabs. Circle the correlative conjunctions in each sentence. Refer to the Notes for Template section.

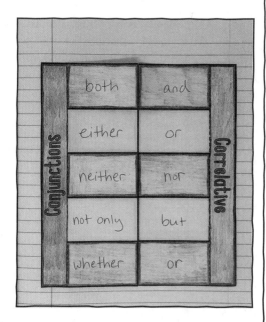

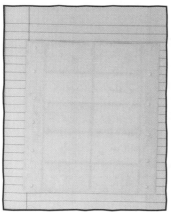 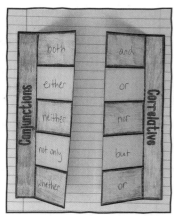 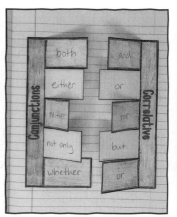 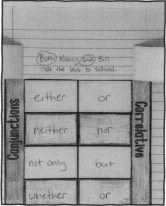

Notes for Template

both, and – *Both* Nancy *and* Bill rode the bus to school.
either, or – Tonight, I will cook *either* spaghetti *or* pizza.
neither, nor – The bench is *neither* in the living room *nor* in the bedroom.
not only, but – Julian is *not only* smart, *but* funny as well.
whether, or – I'm not sure *whether* Sam will stay here *or* go to Egypt.

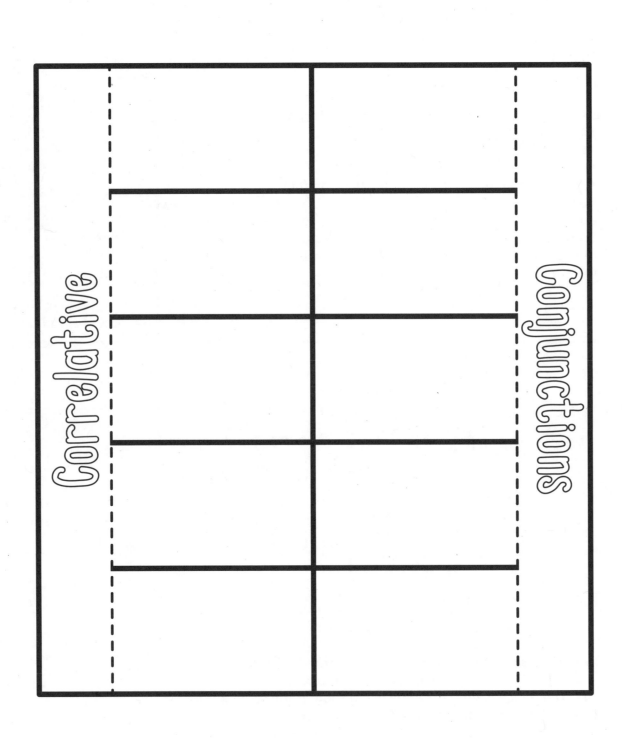

Correlative

Conjunctions

INTERACTIVE GRAMMAR NOTEBOOK
Lesson 9-3: Interjections

Purpose: Identify interjections and use them appropriately.

Procedures

1. Color if desired and cut out the template.
2. Fold each tab in on the dashed lines. Write interjection examples on the tabs. Write the notes in the center. Refer to the Notes for Template section.
3. Glue down the back of the center section only.

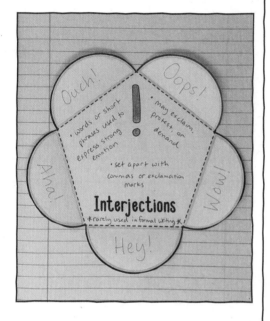

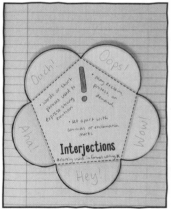

Notes for Template

interjections – words or short phrases used to express strong emotion; may exclaim, protest, or demand; set apart with commas or exclamation marks rarely used in formal writing (ex. hey, hooray, oh, oops, ouch, ow, ugh, well, whew, wow, yikes, yippee, a ha)

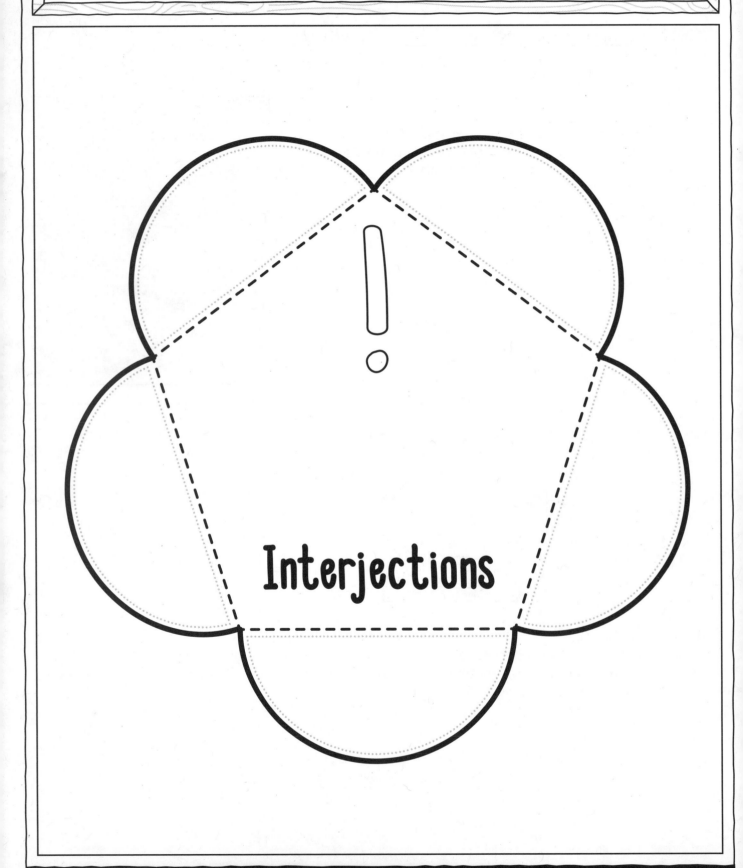

Interjections